Laser Radio Programming

Paul Alexander Rusling

Printed by Book Printing UK, Peterborough, PE2 9BF.

Although every precaution has been taken in the preparation of this book, the publisher and author assume no responsibility for errors or omissions. Neither is any liability assumed for damages resulting from the use of information contained herein.

ISBN 978-1-900401-17-3

CONTENTS

INTRODUCTION

It's nigh on 35 years since the Laser project began, yet every week it seems there is discussion about the impact the radio station had all those years ago.

Despite the passing of time and introduction of so many new stations in the UK since Laser disappeared from the airwaves, almost daily there is endless discussion and compliments about Laser's success, its output and its DJ team. Some of the comments are just misplaced nostalgia, maybe some of the comments are just expressing a longing to return to one's youth. It's a human trait to look back on one's 'golden era', which are invariably one's teenage years.

Favourite songs always seem to be implanted in the mind in the early teens; it's common for a DJ to ask someone their favourite song of all time and then be able to guess their age with reasonable accuracy, based simply on theor favourite song probably having been a hit while they were 14, 15 or 16.

The debate, and no small amount of compliments about Laser, come not just from the die-hard radio afficionados, but from radio professionals and from the general public too, especially those for whom the 1980s was a very special time.

There are so many aspects of LASER programming have really stood the test of time. The signature LASER blasts, supposed to sound like the light sabres as used in the *Star Wars* movies, are just one element, still heard on some music stations today.

This book looks at the programme output and format of LASER in its three main guises and discusses why the station became so successful. There is also an analysis and why the station's name and its pogrammes ideas are still revered today, in 2017.

The book is not designed to be a study of the music of the eighties, although that did play a big part in Laser's output. "Never more than a minute away from music" was an excellent station strap line that really stuck. We know where it was first mooted and that's discussed in the second chapter of the book.

The book also contains details of all the DJs and other voices heard on all three Lasers, and the appendix contains all the pages from the Laser 558 Operations Manual.

I'm sure you will enjoy it and hopefully many of your will be able to use some of the ideas and practices in other stations. Our radio dials really do need a new Laser!

Paul Rusling

March 2017

Acknowledgements

This book was inspired by constant requests to explain how the concept of Laser worked so well. At times it has driven my wife Anne almost mad with the endless questions and probing from journalists and all shades of enthusiasts since the Laser project began, 35 years ago.

I should offer my personal thanks to John Kenning who first invited me along on the Laser ride and to Philip whose money paid for most of it. Thanks especially to my lawyer Jim Evans whose expert advice kept me on the right side of the law and to my wife Anne who had to step in and run our business while I flew off "playing with boats and transmitters" as she calls it.

Thanks also to my Laser colleauges with whom I'm so honoured to have remained firm friends; they contributed to this book in many ways. Some generously provided photographs, and I am particularly indebted to Dennis Jason for many of the pictures seen in this book. Others who deserve special mention are Sir Hans Knot, Martin van der Ven, Peter Harmsen, Fred Bolland and Frans van der Drift. A hard core of radio experts provided information from their archives, especially Jon Myer of the *Pirate Radio Hall of Fame*, Chris Edwards of *Offshore Echoes* magazine, Bob Le Roi and Chris Dannat of *Pirate Radio Memories*. Thanks to Hans and to Keith Maton for proof reading the manuscript.

Most of all thanks to YOU, the Laser Lovers whose appetite inspired this book; you have me a wonderful opportunity to discuss the exciting Laser project again. Hopefully you will enjoy reading about the programming, the people and the often sophisticated techniques used. My aim was to simply give a better understanding of how and why it worked, and made LASER one of the most remarkable radio projects of the twentieth century.

This book is dedicated to

the **ten million listeners**

who were enthralled by

the programming of

the **three Laser stations**

broadcasting from the

Communicator in the 1980s

UK Radio before Laser

To understand why Laser became so successful, almost overnight, entails looking at the state of radio broadcasting in the UK during the period before the Laser project was born, in 1983.

Radio in the UK evolved mainly in the hands of the BBC, whose management were traditionally drawn from 'the establishment.' They invariably held the view that the people should like what they are given and certainly only a very elite few should have any control over the content of programmes. This view still pervades the BBC today and has spread to the regulators (the IBA, the Radio Authority and new OFCOM) and the operators of the two large commercial radio operators.

Despite the clear thirst for pop music, the BBC limited the amount of pop music it played, especially American influenced genres of music, such as "Rock and Roll' and 'Rythmn and Blues', which evolved into soul music.

Whether its because these genres were mostly black based, I can't be sure but the BBC in those days was totally 'white' and not willing to play black music, despite there being a burgeoning market in ska and blue beat music among the many Caribbean immigrants who had settled in London and some other cities.

The only BBC station that played pop music was called *The Light Programme*. Each day featured a couple of pop records, which were parts of other programmes that had long periods of performances by various unknown singers and bands. The BBC had many in house orchestras and bands and a few of these, such as the Northern Dance Orchestra made a brave stab at covering the hits of the day but the BBC didn't really want to do pop music.

Given the BBC's attitude to music and the stranglehold the establishment had on broadcasting, there is no wonder that 'foreign broadcasters' attracted big audiences. Radio Luxembourg was the biggest and broadcast to the UK for almost sixty years. Its transmitters in the Grand Duchy were half way across Europe so its MW outlet on 208 metres could only be heard after dark.

It was against this backdrop of a very undeveloped radio scene, with very little music heard on the air, that Radio Caroline was launched at Easter 1964. Its figurehead was Ronan O'Rahilly who had several interests in the music business; many myths have evolved around the reason for starting the station, and whatever the true reason, however it was certainly much needed. The public loved it and Caroline was credited with 7 million listeners in its first few months on the air.

When DJs Simon Dee, Chris Moore and Carl Conway launched Radio Caroline as "Your All Day Music Station" it became the vanguard of dozens of similar stations over the next twenty five years or so, all broadcasting from the North Sea into a music-starved UK.

Offshore radio stations built up huge audiences not because they were free, but because they played lots of music and had friendly programme hosts in the form of disc jockeys, a style of presentation that the BBC had discouraged. The management and producers at the BBC much prefered the more pedestrian style of programme hosting, with an avuncular elder 'Uncle' figure making any announcements that were really necessary. All scripted in advance of course and typed up in triplicate!

This style continued on its replacement for the Light Programme, *Radio 2*, right until the 1990s. It can still be found today in some corners of Radio 2's schedule.

Radio Caroline's first few weeks were almost as laid back as the BBC's Light Programme, with a very relaxed style of DJing. This was mainly in the hands of Simon Dee, who was the only DJ on the ship at times and hosted programmes and did continuity between some pre-recorded programmes.

It's now said that Simon was simply a stooge, sent out on the MV Caroline to test the waters, to see if the British Government would take naval action. Apart from a visit from a British warship (HMS Venturous) in the very early days, no physical action was ever taken by the UK against any radio ships that remained in international waters.

Simon was one of Ronan's old acting pals who jumped ship from Radio Caroline for a glittering TV career at the BBC. He was offshore radio's first big star and adopted a 'groovy guy' persona, starting his TV show by leaping into an open sports car with a beautiful blonde. After a much publicised 'poaching' by ITV he finally bowed out of TV after a disastrous live TV controversy in 1970 with the new James Bond, George Lazenby, another actor chum of Ronan O'Rahilly's.

Simon was helped by Chris Moore, as station's Programme Director and another actor called John Junkin. The music tended to be mainly tracks favoured by the DJs and the station's founders; Ray Charles and Georgie Fame figured quite a lot on the Caroline playlists as did other jazz and blues artistes. There was even a live performance from the ship by Jimmy Smith, though he had to play out on deck as his organ was too big to get into the ship.

Radio Caroline quickly evolved into a Top 40 station, the first the UK had ever heard. This was particularly so when DJs Keith Skues and Tony Blackburn joined and became the main two voices on the station.

They brought a fresh new style of broadcasting. Radio Caroline announced a merger with Radio Atlanta so had two ships covering the UK and claimed an audience of around 6 or 7 million within months of launch. It was the only station playing music all day.

The two Radio Caroline ships even had specialist music programmes but these were dropped by PD Ken Evans, who imported several ideas and DJs from Australian radio. Most of the ideas had originated at stations in the USA, such as calling the DJs "Good Guys" and kitting them out in a uniform, which made them look smart, but hardly 'hip'!

Blackburn and Skues were always cheerful and spoke like ordinary people, not in the scripted formal sentences used on the BBC Light Programme. They sprinkled their humour quite liberally and often irreverently throughout their programmes and were not slow to poke fun at their colleagues, the music or even themselves. This self-effacing, informal attitude to the job was one of the reasons for the Caroline's success.

Later Kenny Everett on Caroline's biggest competitor, Big L, took comedy a step further and became a master in the art of production. Sat on a ship three miles out at sea meant there was usually nothing better to do with the spare time.

Kenny worked on a better financed and organised station, Radio London. It launched a few months after Caroline with an unashamed Top 40 format, overseen by experienced radio programmers like Ben Toney and Tony Windsor. They quickly attracted an ever larger audience, thanks to a high power signal, slick jingles and tight programming. The DJs often had their chief DJ, Tony Windsor, in the studio, gently encouraging and coaxing them.

Music on the 60s offshore stations

Radio Caroline and London followed a format that is best described as a constant flow of hits and a few oldies added to maintain familiarity. Both stations would also mix in some tracks from LPs (they were not called albums in those days). The music would be drawn from almost all genres and included ballads, pop, beat, soul, and by 1967 even psychedelic music tracks. Some stations would give DJs basic rotation guidelines, such as "never play two female singers in a row" or "no more than two consecutive instrumental tracks" but there was rarely any more sophisticated advice than that.

Many rookie Disc Jockeys cut their teeth on the offshore stations and their lack of experience really showed on the air when heard alongside those more professional. Some radio stations would only pay minimal wages and this was reflected in the calibre of their on air staff. Faltering speech, regular "umms and errs" and a clear lack of musical knowledge was plain to hear, but some stations hired first rate DJs who helped train up the newcomers. Many of the best known radio presenters, and station managers who are on the air today started their careers on offshore radio, which was a valuable training ground for the industry.

Radio Station Charts

Radio 270 and *Radio Scotland* played a wide range of music, but *Radio City* was the 'most pop' station, based on its own Top 60 chart and regular memos from owners Reg and Dorothy Calvert, to Chief DJ Tom Edwards.

All the radio stations published their own chart each week, drawn only loosely on the national sales. Radio London's was the fastest moving with the hottes new releases listed quite high, often before their official release date, only to plummet down the 'Big L Fab 40' as the record began selling.

Radio Caroline's chart was usually called *The Caroline Countdown of Sound* and listed fifty tunes each week. It had positions available for purchase by record companies, song publishers or the artists themselves. Caroline sold airtime to anyone who might benefit from being listed, which also guaranteed airplay on the station. They also broadcast the American charts of *Billboard* and *Cashbox*.

Copies of most of the charts still exist and they make interesting reading. A book of the charts was published by Frank Hoffman and available for a very short time last year. The *Weekly Music Charts of British Pirate Stations* is now much sought after, even though it was poorly laid out, as as copyright holders of some of the material blocked publication.

Analysing the charts show that some stations clearly preferred certain record companies and their labels over others. In those days it was common for songs to be released at the same time by several different artists on different labels, each competing with others to get their recording to become the 'hit' version.

Most of the offshore stations aired programmes based on a Top 40 of one type or another, except Radio 390. This was a 'sweet music' station run by novelist and former British spy, Ted Allbeury. It had a superb signal, thanks to the choice of a good low wavelength and a very tall mast on a former anti-aircraft tower out in the Thames Estuary, off Whitstable; its still there and a major landmark from the shore.

Radio 390's schedule of light music omitted the more raucous hits of the day and won a large audience among older people. The schedule didn't have long shifts nor was it centred around DJ personalities. It resembled the schedules favoured by the BBC for the Light Programme, a veritable patchwork quilt of short programmes and changes of presenters every 15 or 30 minutes.

The pop stations, such as Radio City and Radio 270, tended to have each DJ "pulling triggers on the twin 45s" for two or three hours at a time. When replacements didn't show up it was common for a small team of three or four DJs to man a radio station all day and night, hosting three or four hour stints on the air TWICE a day. Six or eight hours a day can become quite fatiguing, for the listeners too.

Radio Caroline took a year to catch up Big L (as Radio London was known) which overtook them in audience size not long after launch. At Easter 1966, Caroline increased power five fold and recruited a crack team of 'super jocks' like Emperor Rosko, DLT and Tony Prince. They were supervised by Tom Lodge, a descendent of one of the inventors of radio.

With its big new transmitter Caroline moved to a new wavelength, halfway between Big L and the Light Programme on the dial.They followed a much stricter format packed with the latest American hits and a sizeable quota of 'payola', records played in return for a payment.

These had been introduced by a new shareholder in the station, Philip Solomon, who was also one of the music businesses biggest promoters of tours. He set up a new label for his own product called *Major Minor* and also launched a label with strong links to the American mafia called Roulette Records, which had its own programme on the station to promote its new releases.

Payola

Record plugging, or payola, is a term often associated with the offshore radio stations. The practice of playing a record in return for money or other benefits began in the USA.

A purge by companies in the American music business to freeze out new independent companies resulted in Congressional Hearings in the late 1950s about the matter. Several leading disc jockeys of the day disclosed that they had received as much as $22,000 in return for playing specific records and the public were taken aback by this largesse. Several top DJs were fired, including Alan Freed, the man who coined the expression 'Rock and Roll' and gave many of the biggest stars their first break on his shows. DJs were edged out of radio programming decisions and for many years American stations banned DJs from choosing music.

The main problem people had with payola was that the public were being duped by DJs professing to like a track and urging people to buy it, when its only qualification for airplay was that someone had PAID for it to he heard. 'Pay for play' was not illegal, but radio stations were now obliged to make it clear if the radio station was being paid to play a record.

Payola was also happening in the UK. For many years Radio Luxembourg gave its air time over to record companies to showcase their new releases. The *EMI Show, Decca Show, EMI Show, Decca Show*, sometimes followed by shorter segments of *Pye Records Presents* and shows sponsored by *Philips Records,* was a usual night's schedule on Luxembourg, 'the great 208'.

Each programme would feature music from only one record company, who paid very handsomely for it. They were good advertising of their releases and kept the smallest record labels out of the market. New record companies had to resort to licensing their product to one of the larger companies such as EMI or Decca, both of whom got fatter and fatter!

In 1971, several BBC producers were exposed by the 'News of the World' for accepting bribes in cash and sessions with call girls in return for plays of records. The most listened to BBC programme of the week then was *Family Favourites*, which was one of the shows that was axed after a high profile trial exposed how BBC staff were accepting bribes for airplay.

Many felt that although that while 'pay for play' deals are not illegal, it is morally corrupt for anyone in a public service medium such as the BBC to accept payola or bribes.

In the USA financial inducements to influence airplay are still common place. The giant SONY Corporation, recently paid a £10 million penalty after it admitted doing so. There is however nothing illegal about anyone accepting 'Pay for Play' on a private radio station, nor one located offshore and it became common practice. Radio 270 sued one record company in court for failing to keep up contracted payments for airplay it gave to a release by David Hamilton.

Some stations set up their own music publishing company to disguise their own heavy involvement with the music business. *Pall Mall Music* was Radio London's own publisher for many tracks through which it collected royalties from record sales. Many hits were made by intense playing of the tracks on the air.

Radio Caroline always had a strong involvement in the music business; Ronan O'Rahilly had worked as a promoter of such artists as George Fame by an association with Ric Gunnel. One of the founders of Atlanta, which became Radio Caroline's south station, was Allan Crawford, who owned his own label and music publishing company.

In late 1965 Crawford was replaced by well known music promoter Philip Solomon, who warned that new records would not be played unless they were paid for. Music on Solomon's own record label, *Major Minor,* was heavily promoted on Radio Caroline.

Many leading artists of the day first got a break by their releases being plugged on the offshore radio stations. Many were not shy to admit this and publicly thank the stations at gigs, in press interviews and by placing large display advertisements in the weekly music papers, such as NME.

Status Quo got their first break by incessant plays on Radio Caroline and showed their graitude by namechecking the station in two of their ensuing hit singles.

Some of the small independent record companies routinely bought time for all their releases on offshore stations and had sizeable hits as a result. President Records, Ember, Island, and Immediate are just a few examples.

Pye Records had strong links to some stations with many key executives actually investing in some stations, such as Radio Caroline and in Radio 270, where the wife of Cyril Stapleton was a director.

Leading German label Polydor Records showcased their material on KING Radio, a short lived offshore station, and when they took over *Atlantic Records* and its *Stax Records* 'cousin' almost all their promotion was via Radio Caroline. Polydor's offices off Oxford Street became a magnet for radio DJs where they were always treated somewhat royally. Caroline DJ Emperor Rosko was hired by Stax Records to host the European tour of Otis Redding.

An associated Polydor label, *Track Records* whose artists included The Who and Jimi Hendrix, were actually based in Caroline's Mayfair offices, as were the Moody Blues.

Even the Beatles supported the radio ships. Radio Caroline DJ Tom Lodge made a special record with the Fab Four, in which they expressed their support for the station, which was released to launch a new pop paper (DISC & Music Echo) which gave acres of coverage to the radio ships. When the Beatles made their final tour of America, they invited along DJs from all the top stations at their expense.

The Beatles were very close to fellow Liverpudlian Kenny Everett on Radio London; when their legendary *Sgt Peppers Lonely Hearts Club Band* was released they gave him exclusive copies to give it a world premier on Big L. Some of the high profile plugging that Big L gave it undoubtedly helped make it such a monumental instant hit, although that's not to detract from the fact it was a masterpiece!

John Lennon helped start a radio ship for the Middle east which operated for twenty years while George Harrison helped to fund Radio Caroline for most of the 1970s.

The Fab Four with Caroline's Chief DJ, Tom Lodge

Offshore DJs and plug records

As Disc Jockeys on any offshore radio station were effectively 'incommunicado' on board a ship out at sea, and very remote from any shore based administration or management, they tended to play pretty much what they wanted.

Even when offshore radio stations had playlists, whether to secure programme control to build a large audience or to ensure that the Payola records were played, the more headstrong DJs would invariably disregard instructions from ashore. They knew that they were likely to 'get away with it' and not have any sanctions imposed as, by the time management could get word out to the ships, or the DJ came ashore, the matter would be forgotten about.

On Radio Caroline in the 1960s, record plugging / Payola was an integral part of the station's income although it's likely that most listeners had no idea of the practice; they simply enjoyed the music, which was not being played by the only other British radio stations, the three BBC channels.

Radio Caroline DJ Johnnie Walker had such a huge and loyal following that he was sure he could get away with ignoring the list of plug records and would talk about many of the worst examples in quite a derogatory manner, or not play them at all.

On Johnnie's regular programme (9pm to midnight) he would play the night's quota of 15 or so plug records during the first hour of the show, when the audience was at its lowest. This meant that after 10pm he could have a clear run of free time to play the stuff he wanted to, hit records that he knew would build the biggest audience.

The Chief DJ on Radio Caroline, Robbie Dale, had a tough time keeping Johnnie in check. Many plug records would often mysteriously disappear, often because Johnnie had thrown them over the side of the ship! In centuries to come marine archaeologists will find a veritable treasure trove of vinyl on the seabed in the Thames estuary that have been jettisoned by radio ships. The vinyl does in fact last a long time under seawater, although the corrosive action of the sand is pretty unforgiving and they are unlikely to have any real value!

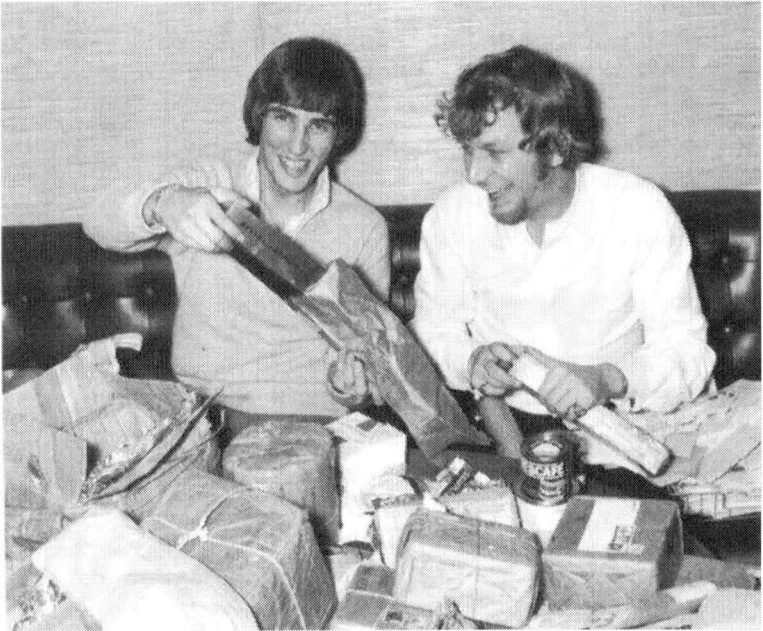

Christmas on the Mi Amigo (Radio Caroline)
Johnnie Walker and the Admiral Robbie Dale

Caroline's breakfast Show DJ was Roger 'Twiggy' Day, who had begun his career with Johnnie Walker on nearby SRE, used a similar 'playlist balancing' method for his 5:30 to 9am show. He got all his scheduled plug records for the show spun before 7am. It was important to do so as, after 7am, he was in competition for listeners with former Radio Caroline DJ, Tony Blackburn. Tony was by now hosting the BBC's then new pop music station, Radio One, which broadcast literally 'next door' on the Medium Wave band.

Radio Caroline's two stations were on 257 and 252 metres (but both announced as 259, which rhymed with Caroline) and BBC Radio 1 was on 247 metres. Both Roger and Tony were to feature again in the story of Laser in the 1980s, but in 1967 they were in fierce competition for the nation's listeners. Both men were regularly voted the UK's leading disc jockeys in music paper readers' polls.

Tony Blackburn was severely hampered by the BBC's punitive 'needle time' arrangements it had with the Musicians' Union. The situation was so dire that the BBC resorted to having disc jockeys sing some of the hit songs of the day themselves with musicians brought in especially for the job. Tony was quite an accomplished vocalist who had released several records without any commercial success. The DJ who followed him on Radio 1 in the morning was an old crooner who had enjoyed hits in the fifties. Jimmy Young was a lovely man, but at over forty was well out of touch with young people and his programmes on Radio 1 must have been a great boost to Radio Caroline's listening figures at that time of day.

Roger Day was also hampered by having a quota of about 20 'plug records' scheduled to be played in his breakfast show, which was always "bold, bright bubbly and bouncy", a bit like Roger himself!

Roger regularly featured tracks from his favourite group the Beach Boys who he religiously played every morning at 8am. Like most other Radio Caroline DJs, Roger loved the music and didn't want to put off his listeners by playing any plug records at peak time.

After Radio Caroline returned in the 1970s the ship was even more remote and the management even weaker. Wages for disc jockeys dwindled down to a situation where only the stars were ever paid. This resulted in near anarchy in programming terms, with the few 'plug records' often failing to be spun, unless the DJ totally approved of them.

Laser's grandfather appears

A month after Radio Caroline's 'relaunch' with a more powerful transmitter on a new wavelength, a new station called *Swinging Radio England* showed up. This station is thought by many in the UK radio industry to have been 'the Granddaddy' of Laser. It was certainly the first taste that Brits had of true "all American hit radio" presented in a professional manner.

It was an American funded ship with even more power; not one but TWO radio stations each capable of the same power as Caroline and Big L and a team of the hottest DJs recruited from stations in Miami and Georgia. 'Boss jocks' Larry Dean, Ron O'Quinn and Jerry Smethwick were a breath of fresh air to British listeners.

SRE recruited and trained two newbie DJs from England. Johnnie Walker and Roger Day, who became two of the best known DJs in England and are both still broadcasting fifty years later. Indeed, both still use the same name ID jingles that SRE commissioned to launch their careers in 1966!

**Original 'Boss Jocks' on SRE
(Johnnie and Roger on the right)**

Swinging Radio England used a package of sung jingles to reinforce its station sound, which was very upbeat, bright and bouncy. The first jingles they used came from a company in Dallas called *Promotion And Marketing Services*. The package was PAMS series 27, known as "the Jet Set".

The *Jet Set* package has been much copied over the last fifty years by other stations. The entire package was played on the first day of test transmissions, over the air, without any interjection or interuption from the DJs.

Radio Caroline DJs were tuned in and being just a mile away they got excellent reception so were able to record the whole *Jet Set* package. They re-edited the cuts overnight, cutting out the Radio England ID and imposing the Caroline name onto them. For the next week the Caroline DJs, especially Empereror Rosko and Tony Blackburn went wild and used SRE's jingle package with gay abandon. Listeners assumed when SRE launched that they had stolen Radio Caroline's jingles, when in fact it was the other way round.

SRE had to hastily get a new set of jingles and they chose the *Thatman* series from a small company in Texas called Spot Creations. It parodied the then very popular Batman TV series but because copyright on the Batman name prevented using that, it became 'Thatman', which sounded a lot like Batman anyway!

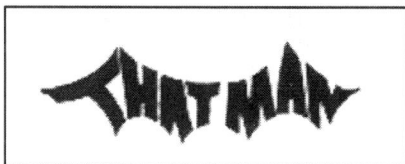

The Thatman jingles were copied by other stations too; Radio 270 in Yorkshire used the entire package, especially the instrumental beds, which had found their way up the coast from the SRE ship in the bag of one of the itinerant DJs on the seemingly never-ending carousel of DJs, wandering from station to station.

Radio England was bold, bright and brash, fast-moving and energetic. It was born into an already highly competitive battle being waged between Radio London and Radio

Caroline, who also had half a dozen other stations competing for a slice of the lucrative cake, whose ingredients were record plugs and spot commercials. Takeover rumours were rife, one centred around first Radio Caroline and later Big L taking over Radio City, which ended in the shooting of its manager.

The British Government felt compelled to act once they realised what high stakes were being played for, and that violence had broken out, even though it was an isolated incident in a sleepy Essex village). They admitted that they were powerless to act so long as the radio stations were outside British Territorial Waters.

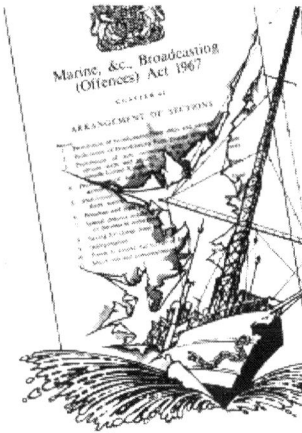

Simply moving the UK's jurisdictions would not have worked, so a piece of legislation was hurried through Parliament. The *Marine etc Broadcasting Offences Act* was swiftly passed and although it was seriously flawed it scared off most of the half-hearted operators.

All the act did was make life difficult by stopping supplies and advertising revenues from the UK. It was easy to get around the problems – supplies from other countries were an easy solution.

The Isle of Man, where one of Radio Caroline's ships was moored objected to having the Marine Offences Act imposed on it by the use of the Queen's prerogative. The tiny island's 50,000 residents, halfway between England and Ireland, threatened to declare UDI (Unilateral Declation of Independence) just as the former colony of Rhodesia had done the previous year. The MoA was the most damaging piece of legislation, and really did preciptate a constitutional crisis, as well as displease millions of radio listeners.

Clearly simply removing the many pop stations that now circled the UK's coast was likely to be very unpopular. To help soothe pop fans, the BBC was ordered to start a pop music service, which it did, rather begrudgingly, six weeks after the new law came in. BBC Radio One hired a couple of dozen DJs, most of them from the radio ships. Copying Caroline, the BBC took a jingle package previously used by Radio London, although they did pay the copyright fees for the cuts!

Radio Caroline continued with its service covering most of the British Isles from two ships (one east of London and the other near the Isle of Man) though it became a shadow of its former self and struggled to get supplies to the ships and closed for a while once revenues dwindled. For a week in 1970 it broadcast from the Radio North Sea ship, urging listeners to support the Conservatives if they wanted commercial radio in the UK.

In the 1970s, the UK introduced a limited network of local commercial stations which took away more of Radio Caroline's DJs, revenues and most damaging of all, many of her listeners. With UK revenues all but lost, Radio Caroline's DJs moved over to an "all album" format. The largely volunteer crew of DJs usually played whatever they wanted, many tracks often this seemed to be chosen simply for their own amusement. Only the stalwart rock music supporters continued listening to the ship's broadcasts, although it could still be heard over a huge swathe of southern and eastern England and after dark drew listeners from all over Europe.

Radio Caroline survived by renting out prime air time to Dutch broadcasters until the ship sank in 1980.

It took Caroline three years to get a new ship to sea but the wait was well worth it as the Ross Revenge was such a mighty and imposing vessel. Many however thought they would never get it together and millions of dollars of American backing was siphoned off. The professionals recruited by the station all left and it was into the void after the ship's loss that the idea for Laser was born. Before that, its important to understand radio formats.

Radio Formats

A radio format, or programming genre describes the overall content heard on a station. Over the years, formats have evolved and new ones have been introduced. The Format will include the overall type of programming, in particular the music. There are currently over two hundred different music formats in use in American radio for the various genres, sub genres and smaller derivations and niches.

The main formats appropriate in the UK would be Top 40 Pop, RnB, Country, Easy Listening, Rock and so on. All news, talk (phone ins), Sport, Business etc are other commonly found 'formats'. A fuller list of music geners and radio formats can be found on the World of Radio web site (*worldofradio.co.uk*).

The most successful radio stations in North America since the late 1950s have been those that followed a strict format of only one type of music. Pop, rock, urban, were the main genres while the style of presentation and incidental music gave a station its overall 'sound'.

Successful stations use 'hot clocks' to ensure that the music tracks and other items are distributed with a uniform level of consistency. Clocks map out a typical hour with different programme components. They indicate to the host when certain types of track are played, when the all important commercials are to be aired, when the DJ is permitted to talk, and so on. Some format clocks will show when jingles can be played, as did Laser, and all will have set times that stipulate the times of commercial breaks.

Advertising agents can access a radio station's clock and insert commercials to certain slots – the best ones are invariably immediately after the best known hits are playing as psychology studies of radio listeners shows that these are when the audience is at its most receptive. Laser seems to have been one of the first radio stations in Europe to use a

'Hot Clock' to schedule music throughout its day; the Laser Hot Clock is discussed in Chapter 3.

Two clocks better than one!

Laser implemented a dual 'Hot Clock' system for Laser 558. This is not one but TWO hot clocks, used alternately for odd and even hours. It accommodated a wider range of music. Radio professionals could see that British listeners were more likely to becomed bored with a predictable and tight format of song rotation produced by a clock repeated every hour.

The other major part of almost every radio stations output is governed by a playlist. This is a continually evolving list of tracks that show most (and in some cases ALL) of the music items that the DJs are authorised to play on a radio station. Some stations will have several lists, often known as an A list, a B List and 'other'. The A list will include the hottest new songs from the current chart, generally songs that are 'risers' and are still gaining in popularity. The numbers that are dropping down the chart will often get put into the B List.

Current Hit Radio Clock Wheel

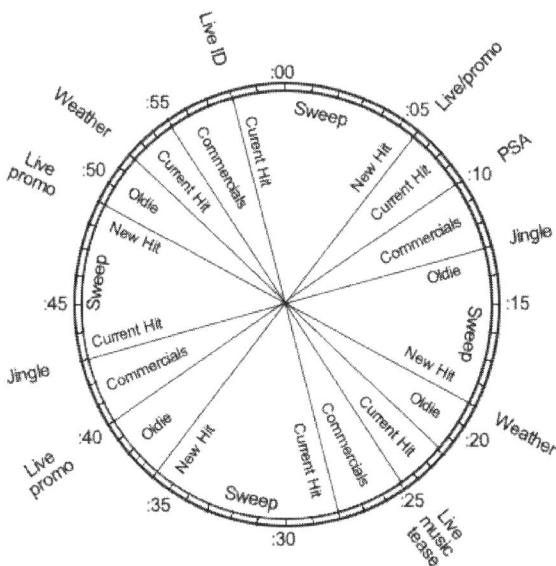

A radio station's 'Hot Clock' will show the DJs the times at which they must play something from the A list, or the B list. An 'A list' track will invariably be scheduled immediately after a news bulletin, or perhaps after some commercials, when the listener needs to know something desirable will be heard and have a reason to stay tuned.

Playlists

The playlist is usually drawn up weekly by an experienced hand who understands radio programming and, most of all, loves the music. As well as the playlist's A and B sections, many stations targetting a younger audience will include a New Releases section.

The Programme Director will decide on a small number, usually five, but rarely more than ten, of the latest record releases that will be played. For the last fifty years the music business has poured out around a hundred new single releases each week; obviously any one station cannot play them all and it's important that a station's PD can sieve out the dross and focus his team of DJs onto those likely to find favour with listeners and enhance their listening pleasure. And thus the station's audience figures!

Some stations don't have a tight playlist at all and allow their DJs much more control over their programme's composition. 'Free Play" segments may be marked on the station's 'Hot Clock' and here the DJ can play his or her own choice of music.

UK Music Radio in 1983

In 1983 the idea of Laser was to build and operate a radio station playing the latest hits to the UK in order to attract a reasonable sized audience. The New York management team's ideas were shaped by their experience with an aborted relaunch of Radio Caroline a couple of years previously, which had also been intended to programme mainly a mixture of the current hits of the day.

Radio Caroline however by the 1980s had developed into more than simply a station simply playing hit singles all day; the team of voluntary DJs had built for themselves a loyal following of listeners and genuinely loved the music they played. They had no intention of playing plug records unless they believed in them, a point that was clearly made at the relaunch of Caroline in 1983.

Radio listeners and the music business alike were tuned in that Saturday lunchtime in anticipation as the station's figurehead, Ronan O'Rahilly, had promised that listeners would be blown away with the new sound of Caroline. We knew that programming was in the safe and capable hands of Annie Challis who was well known in the music industry and had managed both Elton John and Rod Stewart. She had carefully chosen the music genres and carefully formatted the station.   What could possibly go wrong?

DJ Tom Anderson re-launched Caroline in a very soft and laid back manner, saying very little. He chose to mix some well known album tracks with new unknown material. Listeners always need new tracks, the stations sound would stagnate otherwise, but for some months on Caroline the unknown tracks were rarely announced. This mystified the listeners, who do like to know what they are listening to.

Even more importantly, the practice annoyed the hell out of the music business. Record companies, publishers and many artistes were pleased at the airplay, but frustrated that it wasn't helping their marketing campaigns. Some had paid various Caroline executives quite handsomely for the exposure and the flow of funds into Radio Caroline from the UK record companies soon dried up.

Fortunately a Dutch organisation run by Fred Bolland called Radio Monique were much better organized and launched another service from the Caroline ship. It was Radio Monique's carriage fees that covered all the running costs and kept the Radio Caroline afloat.

Caroline's first few months were intently watched by the Laser organisation who by now were busy fitting out their ship, the MV Communicator at Port Everglades in Florida. The latest news on Radio Caroline's output was discussed regularly by the Laser projects's management and growing team of DJs at programming meetings in Florida.

The Radio Caroline DJ's attitude towards singles (ie 45 rpm singles) was eagerly noted in the meetings. Laser's management were very keen to ensure that their station did not go down this path as it would not help either build an audience nor attract revenue from the music business. The entire Laser team were very keen to not compete with Radio Caroline and wanted to offer a strictly 'Top 40' hit music service to listeners.

General Manager Roy Lindau ordered that the station's staff should have no contact with any of the Radio Caroline people, although this was also due to his personal problems with Ronan O'Rahilly. The instruction was ignored by Laser who visited the Caroline ship every few days using an inflatable RIB boat. They were after all their closest neighbours and often helped each other.

Laser's Lindau had insisted that the main 'on air' studio on Laser's radio ship was not equipped with turntables; all music was to be played in from NAB cartridges. This would make a lot of extra work, but would be a boon to operation as it meant a tighter level of control could be maintained over the music played. Only an authorised programme manager would be allowed to control the music and must follow New York's instructions were that only hit singles or the latest releases be played.

Radio Caroline's listeners soon became a bit mystified – where was the excitement of the Radio Caroline they remembered? The big problem here was that the media hype had been so huge and consequently people had very high expectations from the relaunched Radio Caroline.

In fact it was a bit of a wonder that the station managed to get on the air at all; the ship had left the Spanish harbour in a bit of a hurry. The studio had originally been built into a portable building on the aft deck so all the kit had to be hurriedly brought inside the ship and refitted. The main studios were hastily constructed up by the bridge.

The station did attract an audience in the south east of England where its strong signal became heard in taxis, shops and pubs and hairdressers everywhere.

The total audience figures were undoubtedly good, but Caroline intentionally didn't make big waves. It developed its own audience of those who wanted their imaginations stretching musically, and played the more adult artistes' music, rather than the 'new romantic' artistes and teeny pop music that was then filling the Singles Chart.

Meaningful Speech

Originally skeptical that a renegade new station on a boat could attract an audience, the American DJs would not believe that the UK's top radio stations were limited to the amount of music they could play, to a mere 50% of air time. The remainder of airtime had to be filled with 'meaningful speech' according to the rules laid down by the *Independent Broadcasting Authority*.

The UK's local radio stations (there were no regional or national commercial stations, just local licenses) were overseen by the Independent Broadcasting Authority (IBA) to produce a full range of speech content, including hour-long documentaries, regular features, extended news programmes and phone- ins.

A wide range of specialist music was also a requirement and the stations' schedules had to include a full range of separate genre specialist music programmes. These usually included classical, country, jazz, folk, rock, so-called 'ethnic' and more. This form of programming was mandatory until the Broadcasting Act 1990 which signalled the start of deregulation. Much of the content of that act incorporated the lessons learned from the success of Laser.

Dialogue by disc jockeys about the music, requests and commercials did not count towards 'meaningful speech' so the ILR stations had become bogged down with lengthy phone ins and interviews about all manner of subjects that had little interest to most listeners.

Needle Time

As well as a quota of meaningful speech, UK radio stations were severely limited by music copyright regulations which allowed only seven hours of record plays on BBC Radio 1, nine hours for the ILR stations and a miserly one hour a day for BBC local radio stations.

The rates demanded by the copyright holders (PPL and PRS) for playing commercially recorded music on the air were pretty punitive and not only had an element of a price per play, but also a percentage (between 12 and 15%) of a radio station's advertising revenues.

Many stations would use 'library music', which was non-copyrighted and didn't count towards a station's 'needle time' allowance so could help fill minutage. Effectively, the library music (mostly instrumentals) were used to waste the time until the next record was scheduled!

The BBC resorted to a strange arrangement of unreleased commercial recordings from Canadian artistes and regularly cleared out the huge stock it held. John Ross-Barnard, a former offshore DJ who did continuity at BBC TV build up a huge library of them in his garage.

Offshore stations of course were not subject to any of the rules endured by land based stations as they were beyond the jurisdiction of the regular laws and petty regulations. Some offshore stations had offered to pay needle time royalties. Negotiations had been held and cheques changed hands but there was no legal obligation on stations broadcasting from the high seas.

This meant the stations at sea were free to programme what they thought would attract most listeners.

LASER 730
and the 729 test transmissions

Laser Programme Meetings

The first programme meetings for Laser were held in the boardroom at *Tracor Marine* and generally lasted a couple of hours. They were chaired by Roy Lindau as General Manager who flew down especially for them.

The regular attendees were Chief DJ Rick Harris, Programme and Music Consultant Scott Randall, Head of UK operations Paul Hodge, Paul Rusling as Engineering Consultant who had also worked as a DJ in clubs in the UK and on Radio Caroline and the new Laser DJs so far recruited.

It had been decided that the team of DJs and crew of the station would all be American citizens, in order to be seen to comply with the law. This was the advice of a Queens Counsel, whose opinion had been sought. They said that the UK's Marine Offences Act forbade British citizens from taking part in broadcasting at sea, but British law did not apply to foreigners on a foreign flagged vessel. It was very important in getting advertising, the station had to be seen to be legal.

The Laser team included DJs and radio station managers with many years of broadcast operation and management. As such they were very aware of what kind of format would attract the maximum audience. The station would emulate the top rated stations in major US markets, the largest cities. These stations were generally very fast paced concentrating on the hottest 15 or so hits from a local record sales top 40 with some 'recurrents' added and occasionally a 'Laser memory jerker', a very old track from the 1960s.

The key to delivery was to maintain forward momentum with regular 'billboarding' of upcoming music, as a teaser to entice listeners to stay listening, as 'very soon we will be playing that song you are wanting to hear."

I explained to my new American friends how my own interest in radio had been fired as a thirteen year old by an American station broadcast from a ship in the North Sea.

Swinging Radio England had been a fast moving station playing the latest hits and had a team of fast talking DJs imported from Miami. Larry Dean, Ron O'Quinn and Jerry Smithick had schooled British new boys Johnnie Walker and Roger Day in up-tempo US Top 40 presentation; as a result they had become firm favourites of many radio listeners since.

"They were very talented and razor keen," says Ron O'Quinn about his English DJ discoveries over fifty years later. "I always believed if you surrounded yourself with talented people it would make you look good. I told my employees that if they didn't want my job then I didn't need them to work for me. I wanted them to learn and then get better than me. Not only were Johnnie and Roger both very talented but they both listened and learned."

Ron believed in the KISS theory - KEEP IT SIMPLE STUPID. "Make your show sound fun and exciting and listeners will attach themselves to you," was what he told all the DJs he hired on SRE.

There seemed little reason to me why Laser couldn't use the format again to attract listeners. Radio England had been way ahead of its time and was often cited as one of the most exciting radio station in the 1960s. It was still talked about in the eighties.

SRE had only closed down due to management ineptitude, failing to sell airtime. This had been foolishly contracted out to *Pearl and Dean,* a company who only sold cinema advertising and who knew nothing about radio.

STRAP LINES & SLOGANS

These all important slogans used as often as possible in links were discussed often in the programming meetings. Strap lines, or station slogans as they get called at some UK stations, are important to make a radio station memorable.

Strap lines were not used much in the UK in the 1980s and Laser was keen to not repeat SRE's mistake in 1966 of making the station sound too Americanised to Europeans. Everyone was keen that the strap lines should summarise the station's output.

In recent years these have become much maligned as they are often fatuous, misleading and don't exactly "do what it says on the tin".

A good example is a UK network which claims to offer a "greatest variety of music". Nonsense! The number of unique tracks it plays as a percentage of the total number of tracks, shows that it has one of the lowest varieties of music on the dial! Its listeners could make a good case for being mis-sold.

It's important to choose the right words to attract listeners, and Laser took care to ensure that the slogans did not jar too much with British listeners.

-Where the hits just keep on coming

- Home of the hits

- All the hits, all the time

- All Europe Radio

- Where music is never more than a minute away.

Jingle Jangle

There was much debate as to whether jingles were desirable or were "old hat'. Many stations in the USA had dropped musical sung jingles as the few suppliers had inflated prices so much most stations couldn't afford them, only the biggests stations could.

Rusling urged that suitable jingles be sourced but both companies who had made the SRE jingles had gone out of business. Rick Harris said he could put some more up to date jingles together and a couple of libraries of production elements were ordered from *Valentino's* and Dan O'Day's *LA Air Force* company. These included the iconic 'laser blasts' and various music beds which became well known to millions of radio listeners.

One early edict of Roy Lindau's that was quashed was that there would never be any mention of where the station was broadcasting from. Roy suggested that there should be no mention of the ship, or that they were at sea, or where exactly the ship was! Fortunately this idea was defeated by the English contingent, who knew that it was the marine location that was often of most interest to many of the listeners. "The sea is in our blood and many Englishmen have an affinity for the sea," Rusling assured his Laser colleagues.

The early Laser programming meetings didn't only discuss Radio Caroline of course, but the output of the BBC's Radio One channel and the many local radio stations such as Capital Radio, Essex Radio and Chiltern that were attracting most of the UK's radio listeners.

Laser's Music

A great deal of time in the programming meetings was taken up discussing the music content. It was agreed that this would always be well known hits. The big problem was that many American hits are unknown in the UK and Europe and many of the UK hits would be unknown to the Laser DJs.

The problem was solved by taking a copy of the *Guinness Book of Hit Singles*, and having the DJs refer to that for an indication as to whether a track would be well-known in the UK. The book was much ammended, by striking out all the novelty tracks and the very laid back ballads that would not be considered to be hip.

The mainstay of the programme format was that the station should always have an upbeat tempo, both the music and DJ comments. The overall mix of the station was based on a hot clock that features about fifteen or sixteen records every hour. These would comprise a mixture of current and recurrent hits, including ethnic music and new releases, plus some 'Oldies', defined as music over three years old.

Laser's programming meetings endlessly discussed the virtues of various artists. A big advantage was that all the Laser DJs knew the music well and were passionate about it. All were avid readers of the weekly trade papers *Billboard* and *Radio&Records.* This was in stark contrast to many presenters on UK stations, where some DJs didn't even have a music collection, nor knowledge of, or interest in, music.

The station would also include a small amount of foreign artistes in programming, who had recorded well-known international hits. Examples were Shocking Blue, Golden Earring, The Rattles, Plastic Bertrand and so on.

Scott Randall was sure that all continental releases would be available in New York. He had formed a company called *Media Designs* at the *Media Design Agency* on Seventh Avenue in New York that was contracted to design a station logo and obtain music for the station. His plan was to send music to the ship on a regular basis over the satellite link as soon as the two channel adaptor was installed. (This method was later dropped due to the cost for using twin channels as needed for music being too prohibitive).

An experienced broadcast consultant, **John Catlett**, who looked at the Laser set up just after launch opined that "It's programmed from New York, controlled by a lawyer in Miami, supplied by a guy in England and all three think they are in charge. What Laser needs is someone who can hop around between the ship and the coverage area so they can get a feel of what's going on."

It was an excellent analysis and the consultant offered himself as a supervising General Manager. He was hired and brought some much needed structure to the organisation, which had lost its three main organisers in just six months and was haemoraghing cash on a way that could not last.

John remained in charge of Laser, later become President of the operating company, until the crew sailed the ship in at the end of 1985. He joined the next phase in Laser's history in late 1986 when it relaunched as Laser Hot Hits. After Laser, John became the General Manager of *Atlantic 252*, the Irish Long Wave giant station that was such a huge success in the 1990s, where he implemented many of Laser's techniques.

Wolfman Jack

Wolfman was a legendary DJ who had broadcast from, and ran, stations across the border in Mexico for almost twenty years. He had developed the 'Wolfman' persona and cloaked himself in a theme of a slight 'naughtiness' for him and the stations, and the music they were playing.

Wolf also had a reputation for playing mainly black music, which at that time was played only by black music stations. Many listeners mused whether Wolfman Jack was really black, or not? This gave his nebulous reputation even more mystique. The majority of Wolfman's listeners were teenagers, most love something a little naughty, or edgy. Something that their parents might disapprove of!

At that time (Autumn 1983) Wolfman Jack was syndicating a programme called *Grafitti Gold* which was heard on many adult contemporary stations around the USA. These stations targeted listeners who were beyond their teenage years, but still very much in tune with modern contemporary music.

A lengthy discussion ensued, centred around why Wolfman Jack had become such compulsive listening. His programmes were beamed in from 'across the border' in a similar way that radio ships broadcast from outside the target area, i.e. to get around power level restrictions and 'needle time' problems.

One station carrying Wolfman Jack's *Graffitti Gold* show was WAXY 106, an 'Adult Contemporary' station in Fort Lauderdale. Engineer Joe Vogel had been recruited from there by Rusling a short time before. Joe arranged for the two Pauls to meet with Wolfman and his management and a deal was swiftly concluded to transmit Wolfman's shows over Laser.

Wolfman Jack had never had a regular programme in England but was keen to do so. He had made many visits and even guested on shows on Capital Radio in London. He recorded shows for Radio Caroline but the deal was never consummated.

His shows for the AFRTS on AFN's giant MW transmitter near Frankfurt had attracted a lot of mail, at that time the only way of gauging listenership. Sadly the Wolfman Jack shows were scotched by Roy Lindau and replaced by other syndicated shows.

There is still an appetite for the Wolfman Jack programmes and in 2017 an online station in the UK arranged for a new series of Wolfman Jack shows.

Radio Replay is an online station featuring a wide variety of DJs, including former Laser DJ and Chief Engineer Blake Williams, who now lives on his ranch in New Mexico. Radio Replay has four channels of radio nostalgia that can be heard on TuneIn and via other streamers.

FREQUENCY or WAVELENGTH?

It was agreed that the station would promote ONLY the frequency. If we used wavelength too it was felt likely to confuse listeners. Roy felt that Europeans would be unable to handle two numbers at once, so wavelength was not to be used. There was some disquiet at this as it was common practice in Europe at the time to use ONLY the wavelength as dial position.

The name of the station would have the dial position appended to the station name, Laser. But not quite. Radio Caroline often used wavelengths that ended in 9, such as 199 or 259, though these were often "several metres off' the actual wavelength.

This was in order to use the same frequency plan as the rest of Europe, where the frequencies were a multiple of nine. So, Laser would use a standard frequency of 729, although to sell in the USA, Roy wanted it to be seen to follow the American plan where they all ended in zero, as the US Band Plan for Medium wave used 10 kilohertz spacing.

The station then would be known as Laser 730, but actually transmit on 729kHz. There was to be NO mention of the wavelength, things were complicated enough!

The use of kilohertz came as something of a surprise for many listeners, but within a couple of years the entire UK radio industry had changed to doing exactly the same and in future all Medium Wave stations identified their dial position in kilohertz, instead of metres.

▮ LASER 730

BROADCAST TEAM

Laser's initial broadcasting team, scheduled to be heard on Laser 730, was:

Rick Harris

Rick's broadcasting career began in 1975 at his university station WPLT, Plattsburgh, NY. He was also heard on WIRY in Plattsburgh, WCVR Randolph Vermont and WKZE, Cape Cod Massachusetts. Rick is very well read and has a wide knowledge of world affairs and music. He is also a dab hand at audio production and was responsible for most of Lasers in-house commercial production and making trailers, a key part of the format.

Jessie Brandon

Jessie comes from Washington DC, where she graduated from the University of Maryland with a degree in radio, TV & Film. As well as speaking Russian Jessie worked for 13 different stations and had covered many fomats including

country, rock and MOR. She had also done stints at WOMN (a soft rock feminist station) and KISW, Seattle. She was to be one of just two women who made the Atlantic crossing on the Communicator. By launch date she had became the only woman of a crew of fifteen.

David Lee Stone

DAVID LEE STONE
LASER ROADSHOW

David hails from California where he worked for eight years as a disc jockey, then as a programme director at a local station. David also worked as a model occasionally and as an actor. He has also sung with a band in Los Angeles and was working at a station in Phoenix, Arizona when the call came to join Laser.

Melinda Bond / Melinda Clair,

Melinda hails from New Haven in Connecticut and began her radio career at Yale. She worked at a major station in New Haven, Ct, before joining Laser. She was going to be the News Coordinator and would present a daily programme from 9pm to 1 am each night.

Steve Masters.

Steve was attracted to radio while studying at college in Boston. After graduating he landed a DJ job at a major Boston station and was then persuaded to then sign up for a stint at Laser 730. A health and fitness fanatic Steve was put in charge of the DJ crew's welfare on Laser.

Mighty Joe Young

Joe had spent the last twelve years in radio at several radio stations in South Florida, including WEXY and on TV39 in Fort Lauderdale when he got press-ganged onto the good ship Communicator one dark night in October 1983. He had been a DJ and a Programme Director before he joined Laser and became our Operations Manager.

Blake Williams

Blake started his own pirate radio station at his home near Tucson Arizona when he was only 16 years old. After leaving college he worked as an engineer, a producer and a disc jockey (often all at once!) at several stations in Tucson. Blake joined Laser 730 as Chief Engineer in December 1983 while the ship was in New Ross in Ireland and sailed in her around to the Thames Estuary.

Commander Buzz Cody,

Buzz was a former US Marine who had served in Vietnam before starting his radio career in his home city, Detroit.

Test Transmissions

It had been decided that the initial test transmissions would comprise non stop Beatles tracks for a week or so, in order to get the station commented on widely and hopefully attract an audience. This had been done by Radio Caroline at times and been quite successful.

When the station made its first transmission in January this 'non stop Beatles tracks' was the only output made. Unfortunately the tests using the first tests lasted only one day as the balloon holding up the antenna was lost in a snowstorn late in the evening.

The DJs had prerecorded several hours of non stop Beatles hits on open reel tapes and were afraid to break Roy Lindau's instruction to make any announcements until he gave them the green light. As a result, mine was the only voice to be heard heard on those transmissions (apart from John, Paul, George and Ringo of course!).

Paul Rusling making the first station IDs heard on Laser (while wearing an anorak, of course!)

After the loss of the balloons, a small crew worked to erect a temporary antenna, to prove to the owner that the unit worked and an audience could be built. Only then would more money be put up for a replacement antenna.

The four or five engineers had worked together previously; myself (Paul Rusling) and Robin Adcroft had both worked as DJs too on *Radio Caroline International* in 1973, while Chief Engineer Blake Williams had an excellent DJ pedigree in his home town of Phoenix, Arizona. He had wokred at leading stations KHYT and KRQQ Johnny Lewis had recently been at *South Coast Radio* in Tramore, Ireland and before that had worked on *Radio Caroline*.

Only the ship's Captain, David Black-Davison was without any broadcast experience. He had been working in our pub, the Punch Tavern, in Whitstable. He had only come out for a few days to help secure the ship when the American crew had all left.

The engineering team of five battled for a week against the laws of physics and the North Sea to squeeze power out of a wholly inadequate antenna. Eventually in early February low power transmissions could be made and we were able to begin broadcasting test transmissions once more. The power was very slowly built up until probably a few hundred watts were being radiated.

The non stop Beatles tapes were pressed into service again, plus we also had about 120 of the Beatles best known tracks on cart. We began the test programmes with IDs and earnest requests for listeners to write in to the station and prove to our owner there was an audience.

IDs and announcements were mostly ad-libbed, even the prerecorded ones voiced in Dutch and in German by myself. The only strap line we used was the ID:

Broadcasting on 729 kilohertz,

Four-Eleven metres medium wave

from the radio ship Communicator

in the southern North Sea.

We purposely didn't mention the word LASER except once, when someone accidentally said "The time on Laser is now two minutes past one – oops, I shouldn't have said that!"

Blake Williams seen on the 729 tests

Most of the programmes were presented by Blake and Johnny who both did very long shifts on the air, but they both always remained bright and cheerful.

After a while though, playing non stop Beatles tracks gets a bit fatiguing, even for the most ardent Beatles fans, so I authorised widening the playlist to include cuts from the Rolling Stones too. After a few days we widened it still further to include a lot of Motown, Bowie, Led Zeppelin and a fair few tracks by Shocking Blue and some of my other favourites!

The response was excellent, over two thousand letters arrived in the first week, some of which Roy Lindau flourished at a meeting with the station's owner in the Dorchester Hotel. They came mainly from south east England but there were many from Holland, Belgium and Germany.

The owner was sufficiently impressed to invest a further large sum for a substantial aerial. This was provided by the Chief Engineer at a nearby ILR station after he claimed it would be 95% efficient and give excellent coverage on a new frequency, 558 kilohertz.

This had been allocated to the UK for use in Essex for the new BBC local station, due on air the following year. It was a very quiet frequency unused in Western Eruepe and allowed a station to cover a very wide area on even low power. As they were unable to use 558, BBC Essex was forced to use three separate sites when it launched to achieve satisfactory coverage.

We decided to close the test transmissions the following day, at 4pm in the afternoon. I sent out a huge stack of requests, decications and "Thank You" messages to people who had helped over the previous few weeks. Those mentioned in the special closedown programme were people from my pub in Whitstable, radio friends far and wide and my own family who all figured prominently. Even our cat Pepsi was included a few times, though even being famous on the radio didn't make him smile!

It gave the guys on board the ship for that last day (Blake and Johnny) some material to discuss and make the closedown show entertaining. It seems to have worked as recordings of the last few hours have been bought and sold, and even stuck up on *YouTube* for the world to enjoy! Not many periods of test transmissions are as well known as that one!

729 kHz Test Transmissions voices
The ship was crewed only by engineers during the 729 tests and so theirs were the only voices heard.

Paul Rusling

Paul worked as a night club DJ before joining Radio Caroline International in 1973. He presented Caroline's breakfast show but left when the station abandoned Top 40 to follow an album format. He spent a period training as a ships radio officer, but took up a career as a publican with his wife Anne while continuing to work as a club DJ. In the 1980s he returned to radio and has since been involved in several radio stations all over Europe.

Blake Williams

After building his own pirate radio station when he was only sixteen Blake worked as a DJ, producer and engineer at several stations near his home in Tucson, Arizona before joining Laser in December 1983. Blake was very keen on anything electronic and quickly threw himself into all areas of operation: hosting programmes, rewinding coils and hoisting aerial parts aloft. A 100% radio person who quickly proved very useful to have around!

Johnny Lewis

Johnny joined Radio Caroline as a DJ in the 1970s as DJ Stephen 'Emily' Bishop. He then joined several Irish unlicensed stations and the Voice of Peace before joining Laser in february 729 to help out with the 729 tests. He then returned to Radio Caroline and returned to *Laser Hot Hits* in 1986.

Robin Adcroft

Cheltenham born Robin was a big fan of offshore radio in the 1960s and got embroiled in *Radio Free London* and a plan to set up a discotheque on Red Sands Fort. In 1973 he joined Radio Caroline where he worked on the International service with Paul Rusling, before joining neighbouring station *Radio North Sea* where he was known as Robin Banks. An accomplished engineer he joined the Laser engineer team to assist with the balloon launches in January 1983.

David B-D

David has worked in shipping all over the world and is an accomplished navigating officer and Captain. He was enjoying retirement in Whitstable and helping out in the Ruslings pub when he was suddenly shanghaied one evening in February 1984 to become the relief Captain of the Communicator!

LASER 558

After a lengthy period building the new antenna, the station began testing again in the middle of May and the formal launch of Laser 558 was scheduled for Whit Bank holiday Monday 1984.

A breakdown in the transmitter (it had been wrongly retuned) made that impossible, but repelacement components were hurriedly obtained that could allow one half of the transmitter, built for 50,000 watts operation, to push out a signal at low power, about 7,000 watts.

Thanks to the location over the North Sea and the clear channel at the very bottom of the band, the coverage was excellent and gave a usable signal out to around 100 miles. This included the whole of East Anglia, Kent and the southern counties as far west as Hampshire, and as far inland as Birmingham.

Around the North Sea the signal was excellent along the coast and for quite a way inland right up to Scotland, with first rate reception being reported from the Netherlands, Belgium and the north east of France.

Laser's signal strength and its top audio quality helped achieve the high audience numbers. That alone is not enough, as you can have the best signal in the world, as many stations today do, but if the radio listening public don't want your programme content, they simply will not listen.

Finally on Thursday 25th May, all was ready and at 5am Chief Disc Jockey Rick Harris launched the station by playing several jingles and IDs over the sound of waves crashing on a beach. He opened the station by announcing:

"Good Morning, I'm Rick Harris,

and on behalf of David Lee Stone, Jessie Brandon, Steve Masters, Joe Young, Tim Levensaler, Bill Voigt, Dennis Lassiter, and about four dozen other people, I'm pleased to introduce you to a brand new radio station,

All Europe Radio, Laser 558.

Broadcasting Live from International Waters from the MV Communicator, we promise to bring you 54 minutes of hit songs each hour that we broadcast.

All the hits, all the time.

We shall also keep you informed with world news every hour.

Speaking for all of us, Welcome to Laser 558,

Where you're never more than a minute away from music, starting now!"

Sadly there was no advance publicity of the launch and many listeners were surprised to tune in that day and hear Laser 558 well under way with regular programmes. David Lee Stone took over from Rick to host the second show and sounded remarkably well at ease, his laid back Californian accent making the station sound just like an American radio station.

After lunch Jessie Brandon took to the hot seat and continued until early evening when Steve Masters (Mark II, this was Dan Johnson) did the last programme shift of the day.

The Laser Launch Team

Jessie, Rick, Paul, Steve and Dave

Each of the DJs had done a five hour shift and didn't even sound tired as they handed over to the next jock. Dave Lee Stone said they were running on pure adrenalin; "I could feel a rush of it almost all the time, it was an incredible day, after so much delay!"

"The delays were beginning to drive us nuts. You can't work in a creatrive industry and be inactive for months, as we did," said Dave in a full and frank discussion one night. "We were emotionally stifled by being on the ship for so long, especially in the month we crossed the Atlantic, seeing the same people every day. No matter how good your friendship, it does get under your skin after a while."

"Fortunately we were all professional and loved the music so we had plenty to talk about and agree on choosing tracks. The music, the station style and such like occupied our minds day and night, so we got chance to become as near perfect as you could be."

News bulletins were read every couple of hours, they were compiled by the DJs off duty and were simply a rewrite of stories from teletext. Local stories were not used in the bulletins as the idea was to give the news a national or even an international flavour, just as did Radio Caroline.

Music Programming

All the music heard on the air was played in not from turntables, but from NAB cartridges. The NAB standard cartridges had been in use in the UK for some years to 'play in' jingles and other short items such as commercials. Good quality lubricated tape was now available which made it possible to wind one's own cartridges.

Laser bought around 1600 carts initially and the team of DJs spent hours loading these in Fort Lauderdale, before the ship sailed. The music was recorded onto them in the Production Studio, on the starboard side of the ship.

The use of NAB carts for music playout had several advantages. It made the operation sound much slicker and more professional. No mis-cued records, needles jumping or other errors heard on the air.

It was much easier to control the music, only pre-approved music could be played by the DJs during programmes. Control over the music played was important to New York both for the success of the station and for revenue control over 'paid for play' or plug records.

Using NAB carts enabled the audio quality to be maintained: no scratched records, no clicks and pops meant that every track played on the air sounded as fresh as the day it was transcribed from the vinyl.

It was much easier mechanically for the DJ to work; all they had to do was place the cart into the slot and then fire the appropriate button to start it. At the end of a track the machine would automatically re-cue the piece of audio back to the start, as the cart is an endless loop of tape, specially cut to match the length of the audio recording.

Secondary and tertiary tones, inaudible to listeners, are added to the tape. These enable the cart machine to trigger solenoids to either stop the machine (secondary tone) or fast forward to the end of the audio (tertiary tone).

The music on Laser was not chosen simply at random, but according to its type and age, as shown on the Hot Clock, discussed above. A station's Hot Clock shows the distribution of each programme item, whether a piece of music or commercial, around a clock hour. This is was common in large stations in the USA by the early 1980s, although they had not become common in British radio when Laser launched.

'Hot Clocks' are increasingly complex and are now invariably drawn up by a computer, although at the time Laser was being built, computers were only just beginning to appear and few had the capability to draw up a hot clock! Laser's first Hot Clock was drawn by Rick Harris in one of the Programme Meetings held in Port Everglades in the fall of 1983, and refined just before the launch. That first Laser hot clock underwent several redraftings before the above version was agreed on.

The biggest music category was to be Current Hits, of which there would be six an hour. Three of the records played would be ethnic, which included a variety of Motown, Soul, and Reggae. Three tracks an hour or about 15 to 20% of the music would be drawn from the genre, although it was quite a wide and vague classification; the American DJs were not used to being given so much of a free hand over the music.

Reggae, soul and black urban were all lumped together as 'ethnic'. The split of oldies into three era segments is unusual too, as the UK radio and music industries usually split eras into two (pre and post 1963, when the Beatles changed everything). The UK still follows a decades split, as seen in Absolute Radio's separate stations for 60s, 70s, 80s and 90s.

LASER 558   MUSIC FORMAT   HOT CLOCK

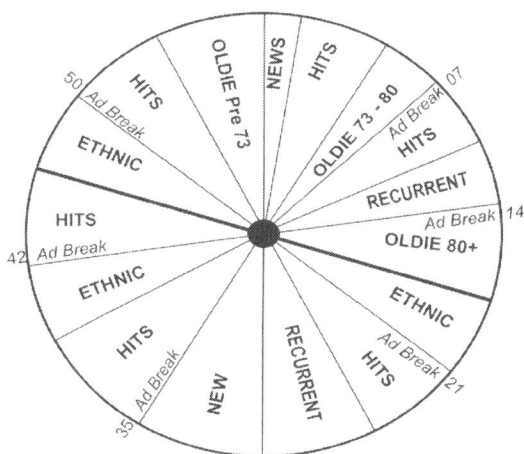

HITS Current 6 x per hour	OLDIE 80+ 1 x per hour (1980 to 1983)
NEW Release 1 x per hour	
RECURRENT 2 x per hour	OLDIE 73 - 79 1 x per hour (1973 to 1979)
ETHNIC 3 x per hour (Motown, Reggae, Urban)	OLDIE Pre 73 1 x per hour (1972 or earlier)

One example of a recurrent that Laser revived was *Relax* by Liverpool band *Frankie Goes to Hollywood*. Overtly sexual and blatantly profane, by June 1984 it was on its way down and out of the chart, until Laser put it on hot rotation. It was an ideal opportunity to lay the new Laser blasts and other SFX over the song at the points where Holly Johnson sings "Hit Me! Hit me with your Laser beams!"

The song just got into all the team's minds and it was ideal for hot rotation, especially as even those other stations who had played *Relax* at all had dropped it from their playlists by the time Laser launched. Some BBC and ILR DJs would not play the track at all and Mike Read had banned it from his Saturday morning children's TV show on BBC1. Mike's move caused a furore in the industry, who seemed to have forgotten that the BBC had quietly banned dozens of major chart hits.

With the heavy plays on Laser, *Relax* stormed back up the charts, reaching number one again and eventually staying in the charts for a full year. The record company wanted to give a commemorative Gold Disc to the Laser DJs but the New York staff nixed the move in case it deterred advertisers.

Jessie Brandon selected Laser's music and was responsible for coding tracks into the correct segment. She made a great job of selecting really memorable tracks and had an excellent ear for music selection. Track details were kept on a card index for DJ prompting and information; a drawer of the cards seen in this picture of Jessie, in the main 'on air' studio:

Music Director Jessie Brandon on the air at Laser 558

The Laser Format

Laser's format was not as complex as those used by most radio stations today but it was well thought out and based on known radio listening habits.

The Laser 558 team did really well to sound so tight and professional in those early days. They held things together really well and launched the station with great panache, with a regular programme schedule and at such short notice. There were few errors and all four sounded slick and together. The 'forward momentum' was good but done without any of the urgency and over-enthusiasm that marred some of the early programmes of *Swinging Radio England*, on which the station had been modelled.

The five hour shift requirement only lasted a few days as Paul Dean arrived the next day and took over the mid afternoon shift, with each DJ now only having to do a four hour programme.

Paul had worked on offshore previously, as Paul May on *Radio North Sea International* ten years previously. He was born in England and had a good understanding how British radio worked and could sound if unfettered. He was an ideal choice for Laser and a tremendous asset to the station.

The station heavily trailed that every Sunday would be a day of *Solid Gold Sixties*, with almost all the music being from the 1960s. This was one of the orginal ideas of John Kenning, one of the projects founders, who had been discarded from the project the previous year. John had launched the 'solid gold' format as a full time unlicensed station in London, Radio Sovereign, which eventually prompted Capital Radio to try out a 'solid gold' service on one day a week on its AM frequency, although it took them over four years to do so.

Music took a tortuous route to the ship; it was bought in New York by in independent music promoter, Scott Randall.

He signed a consultancy agreement with Laser the previous September at a fees totalling $1500 a month, for which he would provide a selection of the latest record releases from Paris, Berlin, Amsterdam and London.

These were collated at his office in New York and flown over by courier service to a Laser contact man in Newbury (in Berkshire, England) called John Coles, who would then deliver them to a London agent, who then sent them to the tender operator on the Isle of Sheppey. Eventually they would reach the ship.

Once on board the ship, Music Director Jessie Brandon would catalogue the music and pass to Rick Harris who was Head of Production for carting. Jessie would then allocated the tracks a place on the schedule.

The music content of each programme was intended to remain the same, by day or night, and follow a 'hot clock' which was hung prominently in the studio. The hot clock is an idea that had been developed in the early 1960s by Todd Storz for his radio stations in Nebraska. He noticed that customers in a café played the same tracks on a juke box over and over and figured that this could also be a succesful way to programme his radio stations.

Laser 558's Audience.

Laser managed to attract far more listeners than most other stations in Britain, from its very early days. The BBC's Audience Research department which produced daily surveys of listening habits in those days, reported in August 1984 that the station had around 4.5 million listeners in the UK – only the BBC's national stations have ever managed more, despite so many of the networked ILR stations now covering vast swathes of the population with their supposedly HiFi coverage, from hundreds of transmitters.

Laser's audience outside the UK has been variously reported as between five and seven million – but to remain conservative, we feel it's fair to just call it a round total of ten million listeners!

The Laser team were euphoric at the huge response to the station; everywhere one went in south east England the station could be heard playing on radios. The station was heard in taxis, hairdressers, pubs and shops – it was everywhere.

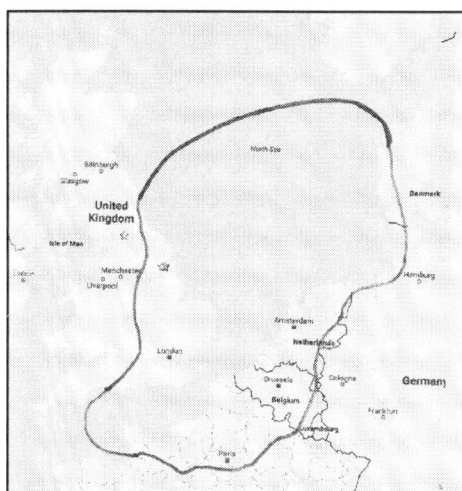

Laser 558 coverage with 12 kW

The target audience was stated by sales agents Music Media International in New York to be "Young Europeans aged 15 to 34 years old."

"Unlike pirate stations of the past, Laser is a legal offshore radio station," claimed Roy Lindau, the President of the station's sales company MMI, run from New York. "Laser is a completely non-European organisation, operating in International Waters."

"We play music from all the charts in countries all over Europe" explained DJ David Lee Stone. "Most European hits are in the English language, so that is the primary language of the station. We do occasionaly run promotions and commercials in other languages, but we want to be a pan-Europen station. There are over 164 million listeners in the nine countries of our coverage area."

Laser Logo

The station's logo was very simple – it was a two colour ship's flag, with two simple base CYMK colours as seen in every piece of colour printing. Ships everywhere carry a whole bundle of flags, each one indicating a particular letter. Many of the letters of the alphabet indicate special messages when flown.

Laser's flag is the one for the letter K, which stands for "I wish to communicate with you". It is international and understood by mariners everywhere. The flag is half yellow and half and cyan (blue) and Laser used it on all merchanise and car stickers, logos etc. It was even more approriate that the ship was called the Communicator, the name and the logo were not simply chosen at random!

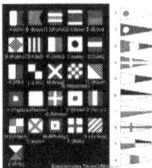

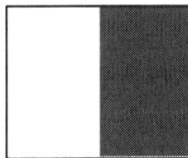

Laser Merchandise

The station made great play in its marketing material to advertisers that any commercial booked with the station's sales office in New York could be aired the same day on Laser, thanks to that state of the art satellite link direct to the ship. Thirty second spots were availabe for $40 to $250, and could be read live by DJs in their programmes, a facility which British radio stations were not allowed to offer.

Within a week Laser began offering offical radio station merchandise such as T-shirts, wall posters, videos and photographs (see the Operations Manual at the back of this book for the text of these adverts).

Membership of a Listeners Club was offered which gave its members a badge, a membership card and the chance to be take part in a daily draw for prizes for hit albums, etc. It's a classic promotional idea that builds loyalty with listeners and helps maintain strong ratings.

Radio listeners develop a very strong bond with a radio stations that which encourage them to feel part of the family. Some large stations even manage to turn this promotional exercise into a profit generating centre of its own and turn a handsome profit from the sale of station merchandise. Its true value is the measure of loyalty to the radio station which is fostered by the listeners becoming members of the club.

There has been increasing demand for Laser merchandise in recent years and *World of Radio* has now made more of this available. The most in-demand items are T-shirts with the Laser 558 logo.

The publisher of this book, **World of Radio**, has commissioned an embroidery machine to be programmed that can accurately reproduce the original Laser 558 logo (as seen above) using six different embroidery cottons. These can be applied to a range of quality shirts, hoodies, baseball caps and other items. These are now being sold by WoR from its Laser Store at:

http://WorldofRadio.co.uk/Laser.html

Team growth

A month after launch Laser 558 got two new presenters in the form of Holly Michaels and Tommy Rivers. A week later a third DJ, Charlie Wolf, arrived and was immediately parachuted into the teatime slot (now a stable 5 to 9 pm shift). The arrival of Charlie, Tommy and Holly enabled some of the original jocks to take a much needed break from the ship.

The programming Hot Clock was strictly adhered to and the DJ's rota included a specific indivdual charged with monitoring plays to ensure everyone stuck to the rules. Being paid properly and consumate professionals it was always going to be the case, whereas some other stations that relied on volunteers might have to give DJs a lot more leeway over 'free play' spots in the schedule.

In early July the programme content suddenly took a more interesting turn as DJs began talking about some of the large amounts of mail that had flooded into the stations since it started. This had previously been sat on by the New York office but once the contents was made available to the station's DJs they had some programme material and could talk more directly to listeners.

It was also at this time that Tony Blackburn on BBC Radio London announced that he had invited Laser DJ Jessie Brandon to take over his show while he went on holiday. Not only were BBC bosses horrified but the Government too were astonished. Tony said " Laser is a brilliant radio station, much more fun to listen to than most other stations. I hope it will give other stations a kick up the bum. Jessie is the best girl DJ around at the moment and the ideal person to fill in for me while I am on holiday."

In mid July, barely six week after the station's launch, Laser launched the Laser Lovers Road Show, a touring mobile discotheque show hosted by DJ Robbie Day. He had previously run a similar promotion for Radio Caroline in the 1970s. The events were promoted 'on the air' by the station, and were very well attended. The station received a percentage of the door receipts.

By late July there was some dissent over music policy and new recruits were being given firm instructions by New York on the future programme output. The 'hot clock' rotations were felt to be too restrictive and not in tune with current record sales in the UK.

Why was Laser so successful?

There were many reasons that Laser 558 was attracting lots of listeners. In general, the programme format was something that listeners enjoyed. So let's examine what the Laser 558 programme format was.

It could be described as simply 'All Hit Music', indeed that became often used as a strap line on the station. Those three little words describe pretty perfectly what the station played, and an 'All Hit Music' format is the type that brings the biggest audiences in almost every part of the world. All cultures, all levels of development – if you ask people what songs they like, they often can't tell you, but there is a great old saying that always rings true

They don't know what they like

but they like what they know!

Familiarity

This is the magic ingredient that can usually make or break a song. Familiarity is the golden word that sums up any period's hit songs. In today's world with its abundance of media, compared to the Fifties, a hit is still a song that the public knows well and consumers via radio or other media platforms. In the Fifties they may have bought a vinyl copy of the recording whereas today most copies are digital.

Many radio stations play excellent music, but don't manage to attract a big following. Excellent music generally has a memorable melody, a strong hook and is well produced. The term 'good music' is often used to exclude music written to a formula that's bland and unmemorable. Often dismissed as 'pure pop', to someone playing it every day it can be very boring. Pop songs are often written for young new emerging pop 'stars', the fodder of TV talent shows. The reason those artists often get fed the blandest pop songs is that the songs don't take much effort to learn, don't need much skill to impart and they don't need much emotion to deliver them.

What makes a hit artist?

How do singers and bands become stars? Why do certain artists hit the big time and sell millions of records? Others who may be musically superior (though that may be purely one's own opinion) fail to have any real success and disappear from view after a short period.

In some cases it may be the amount of backing an artist has, in terms of finance to get the best quality recordings. It may be the amount of marketing and promotion of their record releases. It may be the grass roots fan base that an artist builds up during their formative years, which can convert into their releases getting into the charts in the first place, it may be whether their talent is what their target audience want at that time, or it may just be sheer good luck. A combination of all those will contribute to an artist becoming a star, but there is one more vital quality that makes regular artists into stars.

Uniqueness.

In a world where there are tens of thousands of artists all vying for exposure, the ones who will get airplay, gig bookings, TV appearances and eventually catch the eye of the public are invariably those with a unqiue gimmick. Something the general public will remember them by.

Not all gimmicks work, but many do. David Bowie knew this and relentless sought out a gimmick to help his music along. In the sixties he was a mod, complete with a pseudo mop top haircut and sharp trendy clothes. That didn't work, he became a lot more hippified, but his start to stardom came with Space Oddity in 1969 which latched on to the first ever moon landings. There were dozens of releases with a moon or space theme, but Bowie hit the big time with his spaceman persona and used his royalties to develop it further and promote a metamorphosis into what became glam rock and Ziggy Stardust.

Other artists, or more likely their managers, saw this and jumped on the bandwagon. Groups such as The Sweet, Mud, Slade and Tyrannasaurus Rex, who had all been around for years with little or no success suddenly became an overnight sensation when they adopted a gimmick, in this case 'glam'. Many would say that their hits were not a patch on their earlier releases which had flopped miserably, but the USP, and well-crafted songs by the likes of Nicky Chinn and Mike Chapman sold by the millions and made them into huge stars.

So what has this got to do with radio and Laser? Well, just as with pop music stars, a radio station also needs some Unique Selling Points to make it stand out, especially in a market that is competitive. Laser had a couple of unique attributes that made it stand out, that made it memorable and a talking point. That's just the things that encourage listeners to tune in, day after day.

Many other stations however programme Hit Music, yet none was having quite the same success as Laser, and simply by 'word of mouth' advertising, as it was not allowed to promote itself in mainstream media. No other station however was playing so much hit music as Laser. The authorities helped by calling the ships 'pirates' which help give the station an aura of naughtiness, which appealed to many of its young listeners.

This was exactly why Wolfman Jack became so popular with American radio audiences in the sixties and seventies. He wore a cloak of 'slightly naughty'. By calling offshore radio stations 'pirates' the authorities played right into the stations hands and gave thgem an element of desirability.

Music

One of Laser's most memorable strap lines was "*never more than a minute away from music*", which made it instantly very different to every other radio station audible in the UK. The station did not feature talks and lengthy speech portions, which research had shown to being 'tune out' factor with many listeners.

Almost every other station in Europe had limited quotas of music, which were not allowed to be broken thanks to copyright regulations. In the UK, the amount of music played on radio stations had always been strictly controlled, and limited by agreements with the copyright holders. Laser was subject to no such restrictions.

The station was not playing any commercials, which can also be a major 'tune out' factor to listeners and suppress audience levels. Few or no commercials may well have helped build a big audience very quickly, although it did not help the organisation's bank balance!

Finally, British commercial stations had another 'quota' to contend with. Their regulator (the Independent Broadcasting Authority, as it was called at that time) had a strict rule that 50% of all airtime must be given over to what they called "meaningful speech".

The regulator was effectively 'gagging' British stations and forcing them to programme speech of a kind that listeners had demonstrated they didn't want. All simply because the regulator, with a paternalistic 'holier than thou' attitude had decreed was good for them.

Peter Baldwin, the Director of the Radio Authority had said publicly that "It is not right to give listeners more than limited amounts of pop music, we don't think its good for them to listen to this rubbish for so long."

This was   the 'John Reith' attitiude that had for too many decades pervaded the BBC and other establishment quangos. The newer commercial stations were effectively trying to fight Laser for audience share with both hands tied behind their backs!

Audio Fidelity

A huge factor in Laser's success was the excellent sound quality the ship was transmitting. Depite being limited to Medium Wave, Laser sounded almost as clear as the legal FM stations on shore. Many complimented Laser on its audio fidelity saying the sound was "bright and loud'. In the case of Laser, the engineers had a programming background and love of the music, so WANTED it to sound bright and loud. Sadly this is not always the case with a lot of radio compaies.

The audio equipment was all sourced in the USA, where AM stations use more bandwidth than in Europe. To fit in more stations, European stations are just 9kHz apart, but in the USA they are only 10kHz apart. Each gets more space to fit in the higher frequency sounds. Laser was deliberately set up to let those treble sounds through because most filters remove treble making it sound muddy.

**Steve Masters, Paul Dean and Dave Lee Stone
in the Laser 558 On Air Studio**

Laser played only music from tape cartridges, being recorded while the discs were still fresh and in excellent condition. Scratches were not heard on records played on Laser, they always sounded in pristine condition.

Laser's success in attracting a big audience is beyond all doubt, certainly for hard-core radio enthusiasts who still engage with nostalgic recreations of the station today. At the height of the station's success however it was the general public who were tuning to the station in droves. The *Media Research and Information Bureau* in London credited Laser with 4.9 million listeners.

The latest listening figures however for Capital Radio in London were not so encouraging; they lost just over a million listeners the previous quarter and their station manager Nigel Walmsley urged the UK Government to take action against Laser. Capital also changed their own programme format to one that resembled that used by Laser. "If you can't beat them, join them," said Capital Radio's MD Nigel Walmsley.

Capital also hired former Laser 558 DJ Jessie Brandon, however the Government tried to block this by lengthy delays in renewing her work permit, necessary for a US citizen to work in the UK. Capital Radio were so keen to get around this that they rented studio time for Jessie in New York and flew over Capital's own producers each week to supervise recording the programme.

Tony Hale, Capital's Head of Music produced the first two weeks' shows and later Jon Myer did a few weeks in the producer's chair. Jon was followed by Declan Meehan, who had to 'commute' to New York bringing the tapes back to London for transmission on the Sunday – a hectic schedule. Today this would be done using a link but there was no workable kit to do this in the mid eighties.

Studio Equipment

The basic heart of a radio station is the mixing console in the on air studio. This vital item had been selected by management long before the station launched. It was chosen simply for its appearance, not by any DJs or engineers. Later this was changed for a more practical console with rotary controls for main functions, especially levels. This made for a much slicker station sound.

When the studios were refitted for Laser hot Hits, some British built mixing consoles were installed. They had been bought from *Radio Nova*, a Dublin pirate station, and were made by PYE, a company which helped launch commercial TV and commercial radio in the UK.

Liz West at Laser's second on air desk.

Most of the Laser DJs went back to DJ work in the USA after they left LASER; more details on each of Laser's voice are at the end of each station's chapter, or on the *Pirate Radio Hall of Fame* website.

Disc Jockeys

One of the things that set Laser aside was that all its presenters were seasoned professional, battle bloodied in the art of radio programming at radio stations in highly competitive markets. They were much admired by listeners and revered by broadcasters in the UK radio industry.

They knew exactly how to welcome listeners and make them feel at home, how to produce and present links, how to use the right dialogue and to communicate. American DJs are always well grounded in choosing the right terminology, in using words that SELL the station and the music, and on sounding sincere.

American radio stations take great effort to groom their on air talent, to refine their characters and develop their interpersonal skills. By embracing a DJ's creativity, radio stations have much to gain, but the UK attitude has invariably been to suppress any attempts to be different. The British way seems to be to homogenise a station's output but Laser consciously chose to let its talent flourish. It was quite safe to do so as American DJs do stick to the basic broadcasting rules, which they are all schooled in.

These form a rigid skills complement that almost every American DJ knows and uses from their very first shifts on the air, which is often in their teens at small market stations. Laser was a huge megamarket station, so the DJs were all specially chosen from markets all over the US and strong on all the necessary skills.

In the UK until Laser came along, very few females became radio presenters, much less DJs. The only female personalities on the air were occasional token ladies, who always seemed very subserviant to their male counterparts and never really a full part of a team.

Laser didn't follow the British traditions however, there was never any tokenism and the station hired DJs whatever their gender. A quarter of the initial Laser 730 team were female and in early 1985 there was a time when Laser was practically an all-girls station. They were very soon known as The Laserettes:

Chris Carson, Erin Kelly and Liz West were powerful radio personalities in their own right. So too were Holly Michaels and Jonell Pernula and, most experienced of all, Jessie Brandon who was Laser's first Music Director. She was responsible for all playlist decisions and for ensuring that her male colleagues all followed the Laser format!

Last line up of Laser 558 DJs ashore at Harwich.

Press advert placed in *USA Today* in January 1985

LASER 558 Programme team

Rick Harris

Rick's broadcasting career began in 1975 at his university station WPLT, Plattsburgh, NY. He was also heard on WIRY in Plattsburgh, WCVR in Randolph Vermont and on WKZE, in Cape Cod, Massachusetts.

As the godson of Laser-558 boss, Roy Lindau, Ric was one of the first people to hear about the Laser project - and the first DJ to sign up for the station. He was also the first to be heard on Laser 558 when he presented the Breakfast Show on day one, 24th May 1984.

Steve Masters

Dan Crafton was a radio salesman before joining Laser as a replacement for the original Steve Masters, who left to KIST in San Fransisco before Laser could get operational.

Although he only stayed on board for three weeks Dan made quite an impression on Laser listeners and his late night shift attracted a lot of mail. He used to sign out of his show (which he called the *Swinging Soirée*) by telling the listeners "It's been a business doing pleasure with you." A former advertising salesman he really 'got' commercial radio! After leaving Laser he went to work as a radio consultant in Washington DC and in Paris, France. He also ran an online station called MITA Radio.

David Lee Stone

David hails from California where he worked as a disc jockey, then as a programme director at a local station. David also worked as a model and as an actor. He has also sung with a band in Los Angeles and was working at a station in Phoenix, Arizona when the call came to join Laser.

Jessie Brandon

Jessie comes from Washington DC, where she graduated from the University of Maryland with a degree in Radio TV & Film. She worked for a number of rock stations, stints at WOMN and spent three years on KISW in Seattle.

Michael Dean

Hired as a steward on board the ship to look after the DJ's welfare, Michael was first heard on the air reading out a recipe during August, and from then on he was heard regularly in other people's programmes, occasionally standing in when regular DJs were otherwise indisposed. He had a close relationship with Dave Lee Stone and moved across to Radio Luxembourg with him in 1985.

Paul Dean

Although born in the UK, Paul's family moved to the USA when he was young. Like so many, Paul hankered after joining an offshore radio station and his chance came with a gig on *Radio North Sea* in the 1970s. In May 1984 he was hired for Laser 558, arriving on the second day of transmissions. Paul stayed for four months but left at the end of Summer 1984. He was back on the Communicator again when he joined *Laser Hot Hits* two years later.

Mighty Joe Young

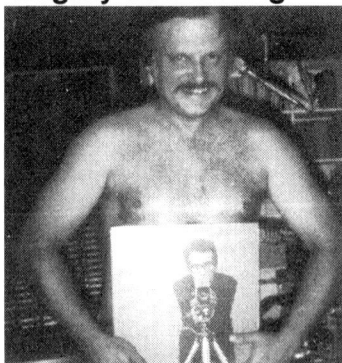

This odd name (after the King Kong movie character) was the alter-ego of engineer and Laser's first Operations Manager, Joe Vogel. He was originally loaned to us by my friend Doug Holland at TV39 in Florida; Joe had a twelve year pedigree as a DJ and was PD at two stations in Miami and in nearby Fort Lauderdale: the legendary *WAXY 106* and *Surf 16*. Joe had toured with The Rolling Stones as a senior sound engineer and worked for NASA at Cape Canaveral.

An excellent DJ Joe had a sharp sense of humour and a warm engaging personality but only got chance to host a few programmes on Laser, as his workload as Operations Manager was so huge, due to Laser losing Blake, its Chief Engineer. Joe later worked on the *Stereo Hits 531* project and lived on board the MV Nannell for a while before being taken ill. He died in 1989 and was buried in Suffolk.

Charlie Wolf

Boston born Charlie also worked in radio at stations in Utah, before coming to the UK in June 1984. His irreverent attitude to radio (and later the authorities when they mounted a blockade on the ship) made his daily updates essential listening. Charlie joined several ILR stations after leaving Laser after which he returned to the USA.

In 1989 he joined Long Wave giant *Atlantic 252* and then returned to England to work at *GWR* and *Beacon Radio*. In 2000 he joined *TalkSport* to host overnight speech programmes and was also heard on *Big L 1395* broadcasting from Holland. He has recently been working as a political commentator on the *Sky News* channel and for the BBC News channel and Radio Five Live.

Holly Michaels

The second female voice to be heard on Laser 558, Holly made her debut in July 1984. Her soft calming voice was heard throughout the summer, usually on morning shifts. A close friendship blossomed on board ship with Captain Tim Levensaler and they left Laser together in 1985. After returning to the USA, Holly is reported to have gone back to her nursing career.

Tim Levensaler

Originally hired as the ship's Second Mate, Tim was given command as Captain in 1984. He was heard occasionally on air, the first time he broadcast was during *The Zany Hour* in the early hours of 15th September 1984. He married Laser DJ Holly Michaels and now skippers cruise ships in Cape Canaveral.

Tommy Rivers

Born in Minneapolis, Tommy worked for five years at a number of local radio and television stations before joining Laser 558 in June 1984 as Operations Manager. He already had a bachelors degree in journalism and while on board he used his spare time to complete his thesis for a Masters degree in management and audience research at the University of Minnesota. Known as Tommy "What-a-Guy" Rivers, he left Laser in September 1985

Returning to the USA, Tommy married his English girlfriend and joined KSTP-AM, as a newsreader. He returned to London to work with United Press International as a radio bureau chief and London correspondent. He changed horses and joined NBC in the same role before moving on to CBS, also as a radio correspondent. In 1993 he hosted some weekend shows at Virgin when it first opened. A keen soccer and hockey fan, Tommy works as the London correspondent for ABC News Radio and lives near Heathrow airport.

Robbie Day

By day a radio Airtime salesman, by night Robbie ran the Radio Caroline Road show and then did the same thing for Laser. At the end of August in 1984 he read the news on both Laser 558 and Radio Caroline, as some kind of a bet we understand. It must be the only time someone was heard reading the news on both stations the same day!

Liz West

Originally from Florida, Liz worked on KDES in Palm Springs, WDIZ (*Rock 100*) in Orlando and at Tampa's *98 Rock*. She joined the Laser crew in February 1985 and was heard at most times of the day as well as being the station's Music Director. She was Laser's ultimate 'cool chick' and not really into the offshore radio scene at all – one of the few Laser crew who never went visiting across to Radio Caroline.

Liz did work very long hours and stayed on the ship for around six months, with just one break. She contracted scurvy at one stage and had several other medical problems, but when she finally left in September 1985 Laser left her high and dry at a small B&B in Rochester. Friends of the station had to bail her out and she then joined Radio Luxembourg as 208's first full time female DJ. After returning to the States she worked at WRXL Richmond Virginia and at WZGC in Atlanta, Georgia. Liz passed away in 2002.

Erin Kelly

One of the youngest ever DJs to work on Laser, Erin joined the station from WVNA in Alabama. She was by then very experienced, a green belt in Karate and an excellent photographer. Erin's last stint on the ship ended at the end of August 1985 following which she took a long holiday, during which Laser closed down! This decided her to fly back to the States and join a leading Top 40 station in Washington. Erin then got into country music radio in a big way and won many industry awards. She also won a major legal case in which she was awarded a multi million dollar settlement against a station after she developed an allergic reaction to a colleague's perfume!

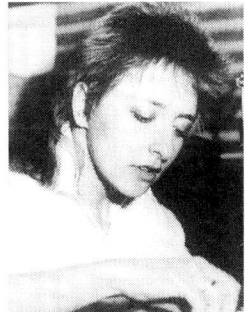

David Chaney

Australia born Dave lived in California where he worked at KKHR, KLOS and KOME. He joined Laser in October 1984 but did not enjoy his period at sea and stayed only a few months. After returning to California he joined KTVD in Santa Barbara, Califonia. He then moved to *The X* in Reno and founded online service *TripleRadio.com*.

Chris Carson

Chris was one of a trio of girl DJs on Laser known as The Laserettes. She was previously at KXJX in Des Moines and on KKRQ in Iowa City. Chris stayed on Laser for seven months but finally left in October 1985, totally disillusioned by the supply problems that were being caused by the Eurosiege blockade. After returning to the USA she joined a station in Tulsa, Oklahoma.

Scott Shannon

Scott invented the 'Morning Zoo' concept while working at a station in Tampa, Florida. He brought it to WHTZ (NY) when it launched in summer 1983. His top rated show *Scott Shannon's American Top 40* was produced by production giant *Westwood One* in Los Angeles and shipped over to Laser on disc for transmission.

Mary Turner

Mary was one of the best known female DJs in the USA when she was on KMET; her syndicated "Off The Record" shows were recorded in Hollywood and flown over on vinyl discs for transmission.

Mary interviewed many rock stars; one with Queen in 1984, became sought after as a collectors item that the discs were sold for over $1,000 each. Her shows were heard weekly on 300 stations and Mary married Norman Pattiz who founded Westwood One networks. She later became a lecturer at UCLA and now lives in Santa Barbara.

Dr. Demento

One of the best known radio stars in the USA with a peculiar brand of humour, his shows are heard on many stations; they were tried out on Laser as an experiment, once a month.

Dr. Demento was born as Barrett Hansen on April 2nd 1941 (just missing 'April Fools Day'!) so he was easily the oldest DJ on Laser. He specialises in playing novelty songs, comedy and unusual recordings from the early days of the phonographic history.

Hansen began broadcasting in 1970 at KPPC-FM, an undergound station in Los Angeles. As he played songs like 'Transfusion' and 'Nervous Nervous' someone suggested that he was demented, so he changed his name to Dr. Demento. Since 1974 his Dr. Demento show has been syndicated and later the *Westwood One Radio Network* broadcast it nationwide and on AFN. Dr. Demento is still being heard on many stations and online each week.

Jonell Pernula

Jonell Pernula (the name is Finnish), joined Laser on a short term summer relief contract for three months in July 1985. After courses at the *Brown Institute for Broadcasting* in Minnesota she worked at KRSI and KFMX with Tommy Rivers. After he joined Laser, Tommy hired Jonell as a summer fill-in, while some of Laser's full time jocks took a vacation. After leaving Laser, Jonell returned to Minnestota and more radio work. Full details and an interview with Jonell can be found in the Pirate Radio Hall of Fame.

Craig Novak

A distant cousin of royalty, Craig Novak grew up in Maine, and began his radio career while still at school at WJTO and WIGY. He arrived on Laser 558 in April 1985 in a blaze of publicity, including a front page story in the *London Evening Standard.*

Sadly the excellent exposure for Laser and Craig was wasted as his arrival coincided with the station being off the air following yet another aerial collapse. He didn't get on the air until 7th May but stayed with Laser until the end in November. Craig and the Captain took the decision to sail the ship into Harwich when all the generators were failing; they had no competent engineer on board and the shore based management were ignoring their cries for help. Craig now owns a small network of six radio stations in upstate New York.

Chuck Cannon

Born in California, Chuck attended broadcasting college in San Mateo. Chuck was first heard on the air at KSTN in Stockton and then moved through stations in several Californian and Arizona cities, including San Bernardino, San Diego, Phoenix and finally to KFRC in San Francisco.

Chuck made it out to Laser for its last six weeks on the air, being part of the crew that brought the ship in on 5th November 1985. After returning to the USA Chuck joined Q106 in San Diego, and became Program Director and morning DJ at an oldies station in Georgia. He later moved to an other oldies station near Monterey in California.

Jay Mack

Taking his name from his all time radio hero, Laser's Jay Mack joined the ship from Boston, Massachusetts. A former student from Boulder, Colorado, Jay became interested in offshore radio when he toured the Netherlands in 1970, and heard Radio Veronica. Ten years later, while working at a station in Massachusetts, he met Craig Novak. When Craig later joined Laser he suggested to John Catlett that Jay would be a good DJ signing. He joined in September 1985, just a month before the station closed down.

Shawn O'Neill

Shawn was one of the AB/ Seamen on the ship during the Laser 558 days and was often heard on his own programme called *The Mariners Hour*, which was broadcast late at night.

John Leeds

From Texas, John was first heard on Laser-558 in October 1985 and was still on board when the station was closed by generator failure the following month. In fact his was the last voice to be heard on Laser-558, minutes before it suddenly left the air on 6th November. Prior to Laser, John had worked for KITE, a top 40 station in Corpus Christi, TX. Following his time in the North Sea, John returned to Texas and KEYS 1440, an oldies station in Corpus Christi, where he did mornings. He studied at the University of Houston before joining KZEP in 1995. This was followed by KKYX Radio in 1996-1997 (both stations in San Antonio).

John left full time radio in 1998 to start his own commercial photography business. He is still in the city running his own photography and videography business and became a non-denominational ordained minister in 2008 and now enjoys performing weddings, specialising in creative, spiritual, and interfaith ceremonies.

Jeff Davis

Jeff was the last DJ to join Laser-558, in October 1985. He grew up in St Louis, Missouri and followed his parents to Tucson, Arizona. While at his first job in radio there at 93.7 KRQ he worked with Blake Williams.

When Blake returned to Arizona after about a year on the North Sea, he was full of stories about the two pirate radio ships he had worked on and his enthusiasm inspired Jeff to sign up too. Jeff was soon on his way over to Europe, but unfortunately he only made it in time for the last few weeks of Laser.

Laser Hot Hits

After Laser's ship was brought into harbour her operators and owner simply abandoned her. The ship and entire radio station were arrested and sold at auction by the Admiralty Marshall. Despite the cachet and reputation, the entire operation was sold for only £35,000, a remarkable bargain considering that well over $1.5 million had been invested to date.

The ship spent most of 1986 in harbour in Harwich and finally sailed back to sea in late November. She had ostensibly been sold by her lucky buyer, East Anglian productions, to an associated Panamaninan company, called *Cord Cabo*.

This new organisation was owned by a consortium including Ray, his friend called Adam and his mother who ran a nursing home, plus former Laser DJ Paul Dean. The sales and support team included former Laser 558 team members John Catlett, Paul Fairs and John Cole. This time they were working without New York's constricting block on British adverts and they had offices in Texas as well as New York.

Liaison for *Laser Hot Hits* was usually handled by one of the owner's own lieutenants. One committed anorak, Paul McLaren, seems to have filled almost every job imaginable and he now has an electronics business on the Tendring peninsular. *East Anglian Productions* technician and audio engineer Bill Rollins who lived on the peninsular was also a key assistant, helping out in a variety of roles.

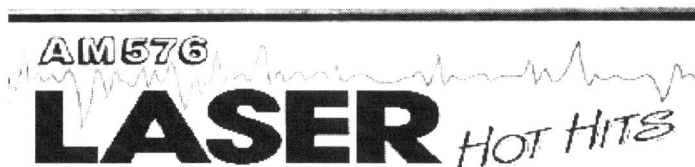

A lot of work had been done to the ship internally and she now sported a smart new coat of paint. Sadly however no work had been done on Laser's most vulnerable component – the aerial system. The array of wires that put the signal was in poor condition and was still held aloft by two slim lattice masts which had already showed how weak they were. This was to be Laser's downfall as the winter had in store the harshest weather seen for many years. Nothing had been learned from the ship's earlier experiences.

Once back at sea, Laser was unable to reclaim its 558 KHz dial position as Radio Caroline had seized it the day after the Communicator sailed into harbour. Laser had to move two channels up the band to 576 kHz, which was shared with a powerful German transmitter. This played havoc with reception after dark, which in winter was well over half the broadcast day.

Laser 576
Late in 1987, some stickers and logos circulated as *Laser 576*, but this was never used as an 'on the air' name; it was always Laser Hot Hits. The **Laser 576** name was going to be used by a prospective buyer (Paul Faires) but he never completed purchase of the ship. He and his backers planned two stations from the ship, which would also be known as **Starforce 576** and **Harmony 981**, a religious and sweet music station, had they ever got on the air.

LASER576

Format

The station used powerful American male identification IDs with Laser blast stinger and the tag line:

Europe's Hottest Hits
We are Laser Hot Hits

Included in the stations play list were several music genres, but mainly New Wave, Classic Rock, New Romantics and the latest pop hits.

Laser Hot Hits had not one, not two but FOUR 'hot clocks' in the studio. These are discussed in detail elsewhere in the book; hot scheduling clocks to help to balance out or homogenise the music heard on the air. The Laser DJs were very proud of their professionalism, and rightly so. Despite being under-resourced, on a bad frequency, in appalling storms most of the time and often off the air they still managed to build an impressive audience.

The station also had a very professional sounding news service, thanks to British journalists John Allen and Andrew Turner. The latter had previously worked on BBC Radio One's 'newsbeat' magazine and his authoritive delivery made Laser Hot Hits' news bulletins really stand out. Had the station been able to continue, it's certain that a very lucrative contract for news bulletin sponsorship would have been signed. It's something that the IBA forbade the local stations from doing but which there was a considerable appetite for in Fleet Street.

The station had assumed a new name, it was to be known as **Laser Hot Hits,** the first of three times that station name was to be used by radio stations broadcasting from the Communicator. In the 1990s *Hot Hits 1224* and *Veronica Hot Hits* both boradcast from the ship when she was moores in the Netherlands.

Laser Hot Hits announced at the end of 1986 that many of the old Laser 558 disc jockeys were to return to the ship and would soon be heard hosting programmes once again.

It was intended that the same format would be followed as in the Laser 558 days and advertisers were seduced with the promise that the station would soon be attracting just as many listeners as it did the previous year: "Around ten million listeners will hear all about your product if you advertise on Laser" was the statement used to get advertisers on board.

The big relaunch was set for early December and test station IDs were aired in the run up to launch. There was no further surveillance activity from the DTI and regular broadcasts began at 9pm on a Monday evening, for some odd reason.

The Laser Hot Hits announcements were voiced by well known gruff commercial voice-over artiste Bill Mitchell, "The Man in Black" who was immune from prosecution as he was Canadian.

Returning to your radio sets,

LASER IS BACK

Bigger and Better than ever before

More powerful,

hot rocking and flame throwing

A new formula of HOT HITS,

recent hits & oldies.

Yes, LASER IS BACK

It's new, It's improved

And it's better than ever before

Programme details will be announced soon,

so go and tell a friend, - tell 'em LASER IS BACK

And stay tuned to this channel!

The first programme on Laser Hot hits was hosted by Johnny 'Rock'n'Roll' Anthony, and began at 9pm on the 6th December 1986. It was a very fast paced, almost breath-taking programme,. He really sounded full of excitement, yet there he was on the air next day at breakfast doing it all over again! A REAL radio jock. Many thought that if this was the new Laser, then it would be a resounding success.

Sadly it wasn't to be. Laser Hot Hits was beset by many problems that first month, including a staff shortage, generator problems and finally a huge storm on Boxing Day that brought down the aerial array. Further damage to the masts occurred a few days later putting the station off the air for several weeks.

Johnny Anthony, looking a bit confused about which ship he was on! He's wearing a lifebelt from the *Laser Hot Hits* ship, the MV Communicator, at the same time as a *Stereo 531* T-Shirt.

A temporary aerial was built using a strange selection of spare parts and by early February Laser Hot Hits was ready to start again.

Unlike Laser 558, the Hot Hits version did have a full advertising schedule, with an ever increasing number of commercials being heard for a diverse number of products. Most were small businesses and the many commercials did tend to make the station sound very cluttered.

The station nevertheless did relentlessly solicit new advertising on the air with lengthy spots voiced by station owner Ray Anderson, inviting advertisers to write to an address in Irvine, Texas for details of advertising rates. Had Laser managed to stay on the air then it would have been very successful as its programme output was fresh and exciting, had great pace and a well chosen team of professional disc jockeys.

Lucky girl Brandy Lee in the production studio!

Laser Hot Hits Programming

The Laser Hot Hits sound was even more dynamic than that of Laser 558. The DJs were 'fresh off the air' at radio stations in the USA and had even more of the latest programming techniques and ideas. They were very keen to try them out in the UK market, although they were frustrated by the lack of feedback due to the ship being out at sea.

The satellite connection was now long gone, even the dome pedestral on the stern of the ship had been removed! They could however communicate with both their own colleagues on shore and direct with listeners across Kent and Essex who would often chat to the DJs well into the night. They therefore had their finger on the pulse and an idea of the latest buzz words, very important for their dialogue to be relevant and hip.

As professionals the DJs stuck to the hot clocks. "As a rule we usually stuck to them," says DL Bogart who was the station's final Programme Director. "The only exceptions I remember were if flipping the occasional pair of songs would make for a better segue or just sound "cooler" coming out of a liner or sweeper. I emphasised to everyone that better segues would always trump the idea of blindly following clocks and index cards to the letter. When a minor deviation can make the station sound better, always do it."

"Deejays are creatures of habit," says DL. "Following a format clock is a natural reflex and requires a minimum of independent thought. I always allowed my jocks wherever I worked to tweak a clock where needed, but only if it made an improvement. Good jocks can always make the rotation sound better than the mechanism, if they're given the chance."

Laser Hot Hits Music

Tracks were dubbed onto the NAB carts and ready in the racks for immediate play if the DJ wanted them. There was also a turntable in the on air studio for rarely played items, although by the end of Laser Hot Hits this was not working as the tone arm had been damaged. No one remembers it ever being used, although this was the worst winter weather anyone can ever remember in the North Sea.

The DJs invariably stuck to the playlist but they concede that they probably would have strayed much further from the format more often if they had access to a larger library or one with more variety.

"As I remember it, pretty much everything of merit that lurked on albums or singles on the shelves was already on cart in the studio," says DL Bogart. "There were about 1500 songs on the master playlist - which was massive compared to some American formats. It was easy to find something more "indulgent" to play just by digging deeper in the cart racks. On the other hand, I would have killed for a lot more Led Zeppelin, Uriah Heep and Doors than we had available!"

"We didn't actually STRAY from the playlist, but there were certain songs, mostly currents, that we Yanks (and especially those of us from an AOR/Classic Rock background) just COULD NOT STAND. We skipped those at every opportunity. To be fair, on Mornings or Middays, I'd say "We should probably play it, since it IS, supposedly, a hit. After 3PM, though a lot of the hot and medium rotation songs got skipped if they were just too awful for our American ears.

Whenever I did these occasional substitutions, I would opt for something American if possible. Two reasons really, The first was that the odds were good that I could toss in a bit of trivia about the song or artist and make the show more interesting for the listener and secondly I was homesick, and even hearing The Monkees could make life seem a little better!"

DL confesses that if Taffy's *I Love My Radio* or *Almaz* by Randy Crawford came up after 3PM, I just said "screw it - I'm not playing this crap. And I didn't! Nobody else on the night shifts did either, and I was OK with that. Laser sounded just fine with 50% less Randy Crawford. And don't get me started on that awful *Jack The Groove* number!

The Hot Hits Hot Clocks

DAY   ODD HRS

DAY   EVEN HRS

The team of Laser Hot Hits DJs didn't only work from the two Hot Clocks, as in the Laser 558 days but used four. The first two clocks governed the order of each alternate hour during day parts but there were two further clocks in use for the night time programmes. In reality the night programmes began in the late afternoon! The clocks had brightly coloured dots for each music type to be played and shows the news (day time only), jingle prompts and commercial slots.

NITE   EVEN HRS

NITE   ODD HRS

Laser Hot Hits had a special **Power Play** slot every hour that could be bought by record companies, or the artist with it's own dedicated introduction. The main issue for the DJs with the Power Play they were rarely refreshed and the old PPs continued, (there were two, alternating one for each of the odd and even hours).

"I remember asking if we should keep doing this thing every hour of every day when the songs hadn't been changed in three weeks. It was starting to make us sound bad, or lazy," said DL Bogart. "I was told to keep doing it regardless. Two weeks later, same PPs, so I told Brandy Lee to take them off the logs and retire the carts. Nobody said a word about it!"

Live Reads

In the 1980s UK radio stations were not allowed to do Live Read commercials but Laser offered these from the start. In the *Laser Hot Hits* days, Paul Faires sold dozens of small commercials with the DJs doing live reads, including the hilarious *Sunday Sport* adverts.

The AIDS spots however were pre-recorded by Andrew Turner and and were sponsored by Lamberts, a condom manufacturer. Many of the DJs were uncomfortable about those spots and thought they would never be run in America.

Laser News bulletins were scheduled to start at a few minute before the top of the hour, so that when listeners who didn't want news tuned around from other stations who had just started their lengthy news bulletins, Laser was playing a hit.

News on Laser Hot Hits was assembled and read by two British newsreaders, Andrew Turner and John Allen. The station owners realised that American DJs would not have enough knowledge of European affairs to make good news judgements on content and they were worried about pronounciation problems. Getting local place names wrong can lose listeners' confidence. The American DJs on SRE in the sixties had those problems with names, and it wasn't just Scunthorpe that they avoided mentioning!

Roll Call of the Laser Hot Hits team

John Allen

Joining Laser Hot Hits as relief newsreader in February 1987 after the mast was rebuilt. He replaced Andrew Turner, while Andrew was away on his regular stint at *Blue Danube Radio*. John came from Suffolk, we think Ipswich. He was a very competent bulletin writer and had good delivery.

Ray Anderson

One of offshore radio's biggest fans, Ray was more a producer than a DJ who ran *East Anglian Productions* and *Jumbo Records* for many years, selling videos and jingles to fans. He bought the ship, restored its interior, adding new studios and was also the brains behind *Laser Hot Hits* music and scheduling. Ray rebuilt the old production studio on board.

Johnny Rock'n'Roll Anthony

Johnny came from Massachusetts, where he worked at WORC. Two of his colleagues there had been part of the Laser 558 team – Craig Novak and Jay Mack and he was looking for some adventure so headed over to England after seeing an advert in an American trade paper. He became the first DJ heard on *Laser Hot Hits* in December 1986 and was an immediate hit with his breath-taking, quick-fire delivery and sheer professionalism.

Johnny stayed with Laser Hot Hits for three months before returning to Florida where he worked for several years as a night club DJ. He was quite an experienced electrician as well as marvellous on stage personality.

While touring with some exotic dancers he got a very bad electric shock from a lighting board that put him in hospital for months. He never really fully recovered and he died in poor health in 2014 aged just 50 years old.

Johnny steadies the cart wall in Laser's 'on air' studio, ready for another wave, which would bump 1500 carts onto the floor.

Michael Barrington

Officially an engineer, Mike also produced and presented several programmes on *Laser Hot Hits*. His radio career began in the 1970s on *Radio Jackie* and the *Radio Sovereign* in SW London.

Mike then joined *Radio Caroline* for a while before becoming Chief Engineer on Laser Hot Hits. He is a first class engineer, especially mechanical things and something of an expert on diesel engines and generators.

After the station closed he looked after the station for over a year in Harwich harbour and now lives on Sealand where he is now Chief Engineer, main communications technician and Head of Security!

DL Bogart

The "Maniac from Missouri" started his radio career at University while studying chemistry. He was Programme Director and PM Drive talent at an Adult Rock station near St. Louis, Missouri, and joined Laser Hot Hits in early 1987.

Promoted to be Laser Hot Hits' Programme Director just a month later, DL was great fun to have on board, always organising tricks and japes. An energetic jock on the air he was usually heard in the afternoons.

When Laser closed a few months later he returned to Missouri and worked in several cities. Moving to Los Angeles DL wrote a screenplay about offshore radio, *Calling London*. It was originally titled International Waters and was first optiond by a small Hollywood company in 1994. That was over ten years before *The Boat That Rocked* but the movie moguls thought it was too British for US audiences to understand the concept! Its had many revisions and traded around several well known companies, including by News Line (Freddie Kruger films), and Gracie, who made The Simpsons.

"Its been 'dead in the water' ever since, but about once a year somebody in the biz comes out of nowhere and asks if my script is still up for grabs. Nowadays I just laugh. For the record: my *Calling London* would have been a hundred times funnier than *The Boat That Rocked*!"

DL then went back to Missouri to work in IT. He is a passionately keen collector of progressive rock and still considers himself 'Europe's most eligible bachelor'! His *Very Heavy Uncle* podcasts are essential listening for progressive music fans and his blog is compulsive too. DL's show recently celebrated it's third anniversary and consistently ranks in the top 20 progressive rock and metal podcasts worldwide.

James Day

An experienced sailor, James got into radio via ABC Tramore in Ireland and then joined Radio Caroline in 1985 where he hosted an afternoon show. In 1986 he joined the *Laser Hot Hits* team on the Communicator and became a very useful crew member and captain for a time. James was heard a couple of times on *Laser Hot Hits* during December 1986. After Laser closed he returned to Kent and worked as a Coastguard in Dover as well as on some local stations. He was back at sea again in 2008 with *Red Sands Radio* off Whitstable.

Paul Dean

British born Paul was brought up in the USA but joined *Radio North Sea* in the 70s. He was the fifth DJ to join *Laser 558* arriving in its second day on the air and stayed for four months. He joined Laser Hot Hits before the launch of the station and was Operations Manager, responsible for ensuring the station was run effectively. He had also invested into the new owning company, Cord Cabo Corporation.

This often meant stepping in and doing on air shifts himself when DJs were too sick to broadcast, or for other reasons. Paul was also an excellent chef and some of the crew and DJs have said that it was only his cooking that kept them on board at times! Paul lived in Norwich for a while after Laser but is now back at his business in Florida.

KC – Kirk Clyatt

Originally from the south eastern USA, KC DJed at Las Vegas stations and at KDON in Monterey.

He joined Laser Hot Hits in December and he celebrated his 28th birthday on the ship two days later. Only slightly slower paced than Johnny Anthony, Kirk sounded very proficient on the air.

KC, Kirk Clyatt (pic by François Lhote)

KC made frequent pointed comments on the air directed at the station's bosses about problems on board and the weather. He left after Laser suffered major breakdowns only a few weeks after he had joined. He wasn't impressed by British food, pubs, Laser or the ship and now works as a TVreporter and meteorologist in Pennsylvania.

Paul Jackson

Paul began his broadcasting career while at college before joining a local FM rock station. In February 1987 he joined Laser Hot Hits while the crew were much depleted following the major dismasting of the vessel. After the station closed a couple of months later, Paul remained on board and was made ship's Captain. He sailed the ship alone from between anchorages and lived on board after the ship was taken into Harwich and helped look after the vessel until a new operator was found. After returning to the US Paul worked in security.

Dennis Jason

Dennis has been a free radio supporter for many years. He was deeply involved with several pirate stations in London in the 1970s and 1980s, including Radio Jackie and South East Sound.

At the same time, Dennis ran a very popular mobile disco business for many years in Surrey. He built up an excellent reputation for his professionalism and still has many fans today who remember his performances.

In May 1986 Dennis joined Laser's neighbour *Radio Caroline* and was often heard on the air as a DJ. After a few months on the Ross Revenge he 'moved across' to join *Laser Hot Hits* in Harwich while preparations to put the station to sea were underway.

Dennis was part of the engineering team that took the Communicator back out to sea in December 1986 and was heard from time to time on the air, though his real role was as an engineer.

Dennis was part of the caretaking team that looked after the ship when she was brought into port in 1988 after Laser Hot Hits closed down. He also worked on the air at nearby *Mellow 1557* and *Big L 1395*, based in Frinton. Dennis now runs his own double glazing company, *Nova Windows*.

Brandy Lee

Born in California, but brought up in North Dakota. She trained as an actress and got into radio doing voice over work. She worked on overnights in Minnesota and held down shifts on breakfast and overnights as well as working on Country, Pop and Rock stations. She has worked on several stations and had a talk show on KVRR, a local TV station. When that was taken over and networked, out of work Brandy answered one of Laser's adverts for DJs to work in Europe. She was accepted and arrived on *Laser Hot Hits* in January 1987. Brandy was first heard on the air during the 576 test transmissions following the building of a new aerial. On resumption of programmes, Brandy took over station's breakfast programme.

Jim Perry

Hailing from from New England, Jim cut his radio teeth on WWMR in Romford and Bath, both in the state of Maine. He was a friend of Craig Novak who encouraged Jim to apply for a job. Jim arrived on the Communicator in March 1987. He was Laser's youngest ever DJ as far as we know and celebrated his 19th birthday while on board. He left around Easter to return to the USA.

Bill Reid

Bill broadcast on various stations in Seattle before joining Laser Hot Hits in March 1987.   Due to antenna problems he only stayed for just over a week, but was very proficient and an engaging personality. He was not impressed with the set up and returned to the USA. He worked in San Fransisco for a while on KISW and KNDD, The End, where he did the afternoon shift for nine years. After six years as DJ and doing ComProd at 96.5 K-Rock, Bill now works at Jack-FM Seattle and runs his own video production company.

Three of the Laser Hot Hits superstars
DL Bogart, Johnny Anthony & Brandy Lee
seen in the On Air studio

Andrew Turner

One of *Laser Hot Hits'* most experienced and professional sounding broadcasters, Andrew had workd for the BBC and in commercial radio. He was a journalist on BBC Radio One's 'Newsbeat' and often heard on their Breakfast programmes.

After going freelance he signed onto *Laser Hot Hits* in December 1986 as Head of News and also could often be heard presenting programmes. Andrew worked at *Blue Danube Radio* in Vienna in the periods Laser was off the air, and after the station closed he joined London news station, *LBC*. A few years later Andrew was heard presenting news bulletins on both *Atlantic 252* and *Capital Gold.*

**Andrew Turner leaving the Communicator
for another stint on Blue Danube Radio.**

Life after Laser

Laser's effects on radio

Laser did many things for British radio and its listeners. The first change was to provide listeners with a new style and genre of radio. A new fresh format that most had not heard before. This influenced many cultural groups and helped drive the appetite for tastes and interest in the future.

The second effect it had was on the regulatory system. Laser proved that the old IBA method of mandating that radio stations be "all things to all men" was not what the listening public wanted, and that more sharply defined programmes and formats were wanted. It was indeed a new model of programming and many changes were made both by the BBC and by the legislation that controlled independent radio later, especially the UK's 1990 Broadcasting Act.

Laser was a catalyst and helped bring about many changes to British radio in so many ways, in particular it caused the reshaping of the stagnating ten year old network of local radio stations. It also helped pave the way for a two new tiers of commercial radio – regional and national commercial stations.

The third effect was the abolition of 'needle time' in the UK. As discussed earlier in the book, music radio in the UK had long been strangled by restrictions on the use of commercially recorded music. In 1983, BBC Radio One had an allowance of only 7 hours needle time a day and it was the UK's only national music station. BBC local radio fared even worse with just one hour a day of needle time.

The ILR stations were gamely trying to fill 24 hours of programmes with only 9 hours a day of needle time. There had been some efforts led by Bill MacDonald of *Radio Hallam* to persuade the licensing bodies to increase this limit.

When Laser started making massive inroads into the audiences of the big ILR stations in the south-east, this gave the campaign extra impetus. From 1995 they were able to get Government support for the needle time restrictions to be relaxed so they could compete.

UK radio stations now enjoy (or rather their listeners enjoy) unlimited needletime. Many concede that this is partly due to the appearance of Laser and its success in attracting a large audience.

Laser's effects were acted on first by the BBC. Johnny Beerling, a producer at BBC Radio One who became controller of the station in 1985. He had helped shape Radio One at its launch in 1967 which had been based on Radio London; Johnny even made a trip out to the Big L ship as a studio manager to study its operation and learn how to control DJs.

The changes that Beerling made during 1985 were strongly influenced by Laser. One of his biggest changes was to re-introduce a formal playlist to the station. This was however partly done to ensure a mandatory amount of specialist music was featured, as had been done by Laser in the station's daytime shows.

Laser is also acknowledge to have helped build the strength of artists by its introduction of 'recurrents'. Before Laser arrived, UK radio focussed on current hits, or oldies. Records that were dropping down the charts or had recently been hits were ignored, which made it very difficult for artistes to establish themselves.

Laser did schedule recurrents, at a rate of two per clock hour. Although that's only a third of the plays allocated for current hits, keeping recent hits on the playlist was deemed very helpful by many artists, as the other stations copied whatever Laser did, in case they missed a trick on winning listeners.

The number of slots for of recurrents was increased after Laser had been on the air a few months. This was due to the station's suppliers failure to get new music to the ship; that and certain individuals' clumsy attempts to get their own plug records aired more often. The diligent DJs spotted this and replaced them with recurrents they knew were more popular.

While BBC Radio One and Capital Radio in London were always eager to play the newest records first, Laser only started playing them when they were already established hits (or, at least, well on their way there). Laser continued to play records as they dropped down the charts and beyond.

This makes perfect sense in serving both listeners and the artists as it takes time for a song to become popular outside an artist's immediate fan base. The most played tracks on stations such as *Magic, Heart* and *Smooth* today are not the largest releases but are mostly recurrents. Those are the stations that have the largest audiences.

The high levels of bureacracy were one of the first hurdles to be surmounted inside the IBA system and that was indirectly helped by Laser. The AIRC (a trade group of ILR contractors – they were not strictly licensees) had copies of Laser's records, such as they were and were able to demonstrate that Laser needed only a fraction of the staff and less than ten percent of the paperwork for a full year of operation than most ILR operations generated in a week.

To be fair, the ILR station managers had been hammering away at the IBA for some time to loosen its regulatory control over the stations. At a major but very secret conference at the Sheraton Skyline Hotel (known as the *Heathrow Conference*) on 23rd June 1984. This was less than a month after the launch of Laser but already most stations, especially those in the south east, had seen how vulnerable they were, how they could lose millions of listeners (they did!) and how this would affect their revenue levels.

The local radio contractors (ILR stations) voted overwhelmingly to "reconsider paying their statutory fees," then running at around £13m a year, unless something was done urgently by the Government about pirate radio. This was sent to the Home Secretary and to the Prime Minister, Margaret Thatcher. Their initiative was put down by John Whitney, the Director General of the IBA who had previously been involved in both commercial radio (at Capital in the 1970s) and offshore radio in the 1960s.

The report by *The Economist* into the future regulation of radio highlighted some of the effects of Laser:

> *The BBC's ability to draw attention to radio broadcasting has not been so much in evidence since 1967, when mounting competition from offshore pirate 'Caroline' forced the BBC to reconsider its audience. The result was Radio One. Could today's pirates have an equally catalytic effect?*

The Economist's report also highlighted the huge differences in the costs of setting up commercial radio stations in different countries, from £20,000 in Italy to £500,000 in the UK. The Economist report blamed this on the IBA's insistence on using top of the range equipment, which was usually unnecessary. The analysis presented ILR as overburdened with a complex business model. It felt that a more lighter touch regulatory framework was the most workable model.

Gold music (Oldies)

Laser's *Solid Gold Sunday* programming initiative caught the imagination of many radio programmers around the UK and a network in Belgium emulated this as early as 1985.

In 1988 the ILR stations were under pressure to end simulcasting as many newcomers wanted to open new services. Capital Radio agreed to try out a 'solid gold' service, initially as a weekend only service on its AM frequency. Eventually this became a full time 'Capital Gold' in November 1988.

Before Capital Gold launched, a new local station in Hull, Viking Radio, had also turned its MW frequency over to an 'all oldies' format, *Classic Gold*. It was an immediate success, although some of Viking's DJs were afraid to be shunted off onto the AM frequency.

The station's first PD however had no problem and already knew the music very well as it was none other than **Keith Skues**. He had begun his career on the British Forces Network stations, then joined Radio Caroline and Big L before a long career at Radio One. Over fifty years later he is still on the air and hosts a popular weekly programme on many BBC local stations in East Anglia, still playing the same music!

Laser had proven that there was a demand for oldies on the radio and shown how it could be immensely popular, if well presented. Oldies appeal to almost all age groups and other demographic groups. was just the excuse ILR stations needed to implement this. Without Laser showing the way, the IBA would never have agreed to any such move.

Not long after starting their Gold service, it was rolled out onto sister stations Radio Hallam and Pennine as Great Yorkshire Gold. Not long after, the group was subject of a hostile takeover by another operator, Metro, who replaced Keith Skues and many of the station's best known DJs with new 'fresher' voices.

One victim of the Metro axe was DJ Jon Culshaw, who was told that his voice was "not suitable for what they felt was good for the area." John in fact probably has more voices than anyone else in radio and is now much better known for his work on BBC Radio 4 and the TV series of *Dead Ringers*!

Laser Merchandise

Interest in Laser branded products and items are still in great demand by radio enthusiasts.

Radio Fab continue to make several products including DVDs of life on the ship as part of the East Anglian Productions catalogue. These are all available via the WoR web site. Of interest to DJs and others who want to relive the

'sound' of Laser is the CD *Pirate Radio Jingles of the 80s*. This contains 30 of Laser 558's jingles and 57 cuts (a wide variety!) from the Laser Hot Hits period. The CD also contains a dozen Radio Caroline jingles. All have superb audio quality and can be obtained through the World of Radio web site for £14.99 (*worldofradio.co.uk*).

The same site also has several different Laser T-shirts, hoodies, hats and other high quality garments available, all with the Laser '*All Europe Radio*' logo embroidered onto them in full colour using long-lasting cottons that won't fray or fade. A useful souvenir to treasure and to wear proudly for all radio fans of the 1980s to celebrate one of the most remarkable radio stations of that era.

Communicator Book

In late 2016 I wrote a book about the radio career of Laser's ship, the MV Communicator. It spent the last 21 years of its life as a radio ship and was home not only to Laser but to several other radio stations.

The best known Dutch broadcaster, Radio Veronica broadcast from the Communicator for a few years and it finished its years as a community radio station in Orkney.

Radio Adventures of the MV Communicator is a gripping rip-roaring pirate tale of raids, takeovers, boardings, government blockades and much more excitement. Subterfuge, gangsters, ships adrift all form part of the Communicator's story, but its also peppered with humour and some "unbelievable" acts of stupidity.

Over 200 pages long, the stories are from the DJs, the engineers, owners, suppliers etc associated with the stations, as are some of the 150 photographs, many unique to the book. Signed copies are available direct from the publishers, World of Radio, at the web site (*worldofradio.co.uk*).

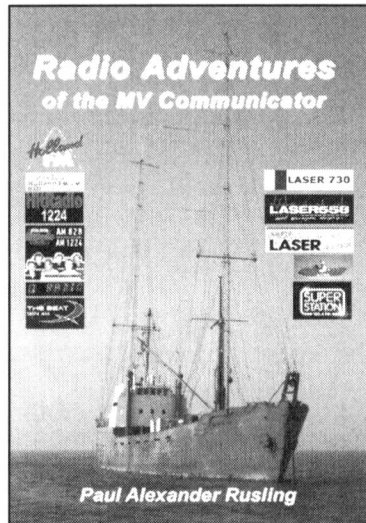

Laser Team

Some of the Laser team assimilated into other radio stations and projects.

After leaving Laser, Rick Harris did a short stint on Dublin's legendary pirate station, Radio Nova before moving back to the US where he now works in IT.

Liz West spent some time in Kent and then was recruited by Radio Luxembourg. Jessie Brandon too served for a tour of duty out in the Grand Duchy.

Laser manager John Catlett headed up the launch of Atlantic 252, a station jointly owned by Radio Luxembourg's parent, CLT and the Irish state broadcaster RTE. It broadcast from Ireland with a whopping 500 kW signal on Long Wave, but was sold to a German sports company called *Teamtalk* after only ten years.

One of Atlantic 252's first DJs was Charlie Wolf, who had become so well known for his controversial and highly entertaining night time broadcasts on Laser.

Most of Laser's DJs returned to the USA after they left Laser, but the UK radio industry has fortunately held onto two of them:

Laser boys in UK Talk Radio

While none of the Laser 558 DJs are heard hosting music programmes on British radio any longer, two are still found as correspondents in news and current affairs programmes.

Tommy 'What a Guy' Rivers is still the London correspondent for a major American news network and can often be heard voicing actuality and bulletins.

Charlie Wolf has also made quite a name for himself as a political pundit and is regularly seen on *BBC TV News*, *Sky News* and on *BBC Radio 5 Live* explaining the American political scene for viewers and listeners, and at a time when interest in American politics has never been higher.

Others joined other big coverage stations for the UK. Rick Harris tried life at top Irish station Radio Nova for six months, and Jessie Brandon, Dave Lee Stone and Liz West all joined Radio Luxembourg. Jessie also joined Capital Radio, the UK's biggest ILR station however the Home Office refused to renew her Work Permit in a fit of spiteful pique.

Capital simply had Jessie record programmes at a studio in New York and flew a producer over each week to supervise. She was a huge name in the London area at that time and brought tremendous cachet to Capital's output.

"A women's place is in the kitchen?" That was never a policy on Laser, but Jessie was a great cook and always willing to fix a meal for her colleagues.

Laser Road Shows

The **Laser Road Show** that operated in the UK for many years in the 1980s was not strictly connected to Laser, but was run by Rob Day, who during the day was an air time salesman. He was also involved with a similar venture for *Radio Caroline* and *Stereo Hits* (Samantha Fox did her first public singing performances with the *Stereo 531 Roadshow*).

In the Netherlands there was another Laser Road show, this one run by using equipment from Nico Volker, or Radio Monique and Holland FM name. In the 1990s Nico's company bought the Communicator and they took it to Holland, where it operated at full power with a new aerial for many years and was very successful.

The Laser Road Shows were very successful in Holland and Belgium, when managed by Frans van der Drift. Well known Dutch singer **Vanessa** (Connie Wittman) is seen here on stage at one Laser Road Show in the Bonkelaar Theatre in Sliedrecht, near Rotterdam. She had over a dozen hits in the Netherlands, including *Upside Down, Obsession* and *Cheerio*.

Mai Tai were a Dutch trio formed in Holland in the early 1980s who appeared on many of the Laser Road Shows performing their single releases live. The group was led by **Carolien de Windt** and sometimes had up to six members in its entourage.

Mai Tai's singles did very well and they had hits all around the world. They also had three hits in the UK, thanks to the air play they got on Laser; one of them, called *Body and Soul*, made it into the UK Top 10 in September 1985.

As well as being a well known cocktail, Mai Tai means GOOD in Tahitian.

Carolien de Windt of Mai Tai on stage at a Laser Road Show

Radio Tributes to Laser

RTI, an independent online station based in Poprad in Slovakia have broadcast many "all Laser" days and even a weekend long tribute series of programmes during 2016. They brought such a positive response from RTI's listeners that they are planning several more similar events in 2017.

The shows are usually comprised of archive recordings of Laser programes as broadcast in the 1980s. RTI (it stands for *Radio Tatras International*) is an international radio station with outlets on almost every streaming platform and now operates two streams 24 hours a day.

In recent years many other stations have broadcast lengthy Laser tributes, including MITA RADIO. This online station was run by **Dan Crafton,** who was one of the launch DJs on Laser 558 as Steve Masters, although he has since handed it over to RTI.

In the 1990s, the name **Laser FM** was used by an unlicensed station in the East Midlands. They used the usual Laser blasts and broadcast on 105.8 but after a couple of years the station disappeared. This may have been the same group who broadcast as **Laser Hot Hits** for several months in 2002 in the Nottingham and Derby area on 102.2FM.

Across on Merseyside a station called **LAZER UK** has broadcast from The Wirral across Liverpool since 2000. It appears to be a weekend only operation, on 106.5FM. Down the M6 in the Stoke area there was a Laser 98 for about a year in 1988, but they have not been heard for many years.

In the West Midlands **LASER FM Birmingham** has broadcast intermittently since 1989 on several FM frequencies. The station broadcasts black music and community information. **Laser FM** in the York area was heard for some years on 100.2 in the 1990s and again around 2008 emulating the Laser 558 format but they appear to have become a community radio station now.

The Laser 558 Tribute Stream

An excellent online radio station that is based on a non-stop stream of archive recordings of *Laser 558* programmes. The Laser Tribute Stream has been running since 2010 and has hundreds of followers on social media with listeners in 155 countries.

The stream is processed to sound like an AM signal and available on the *TuneIn* servers, where it has several hundred followers. It also uses the name **All Hit Radio**, which was one of Laser 558's strap lines. The station accepts requests for eighties tracks via Twitter.

The team behind the Laser 558 Tribute site, which appears to be run from Spain, announced in early 2017 that they will shortly launch a Music TV service online, starting in the Spring. It will be called **Channel558** – clearly a reference to Laser 558.

Laser Blasts

Many other radio stations used the Laser 'blast' sound effects as stingers for many years after Laser's demise, even though they had no apparent link or involvement in their programme output. It seems that the DJs simply enjoyed the spaced-out or futuristic sounds!

Laser Name

The name Laser was used by several small, generally hobbyist radio stations as well as some local radio operators for many years, a practice that continues in 2017.

At the end of 1989 a group of DJs in North London broadcast as **Laser FM** on 94.0 MHz from several sites. They managed to avade the DTI investigators for two years but have not been heard widely since 1991.

Perhaps they were scared off by another Laser organisation that launched in 1990 and broadcast as **Laser Hot Hits** on several FM frequencies, and on 6.220 mHz in the 49m short wave band. The station was started by a group of dedicated radio enthusiasts about Easter 1990 on 101 FM and could be heard all over the home counties until INR station Classic FM launched, forcing them to move to 102. They later merged with *Hits FM* and eventually moved to Short Wave, discontinuing the FM transmissions in 1996.

They are well organised and have continued broadcasting ever since, now in their 27th year.

In 1994 their transmission came from a derelict cottage at Pear Wood near Stanmore. It's only two miles from the DTI's base near Stanmore but by the time their investigators got close all the kit had been moved and only a site guard (Colin Dixon) was found.

In 2014 their 98FM signal was heard clearly in Eastbourne. The Short Wave service of Laser Hot Hits has recently moved to 4029 Khz, and 5800 KHz is now called **Laser Hot Hits International**. Its regularly heard across the Benelux countries as well as England. They have expanded into weekday evening transmissions as well as weekends.

Today Laser Hot Hits concentrates on its high quality internet stream which is on air 24 hours a day. Regular DJs on Laser Hot Hits include Ian Lawrence, Paul Stewart, soul boy Gary Drew and production wizard Stewart Ross. Most of the station's programmes can be heard on *Mixcloud* too.

A recent development has seen Laser Hot Hits International broadcasting on Medium Wave at 1476 and 1494 kHz with a usable signal over North London and out into Hertfordshire. They also have an online service which carries live programming most days and run an active Facebook page and web site.

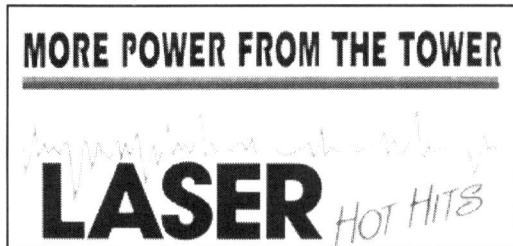

MORE POWER FROM THE TOWER

LASER Hot Hits

Laser Broadcasting was a group of companies formed by Nigel Reeve, who had been Chief Executive of LBC and a launch director at Classic FM and Nick Jordan of Invicta and KFM. Laser Broadcasting bid for several UK ILR licenses in the 1990s, in place like Hull and Darlington. They eventually held stakes in nine small stations, such as Fresh, Sunshine, Bath and Brunel. All made a loss and were sold after Nigel's *Laser Broadcasting* went into administration in 2008.

LaserRadio.net

This organisation was active around the turn of the millennium and heard across Europe via brokered airtime on a variety of relay transmitters. They also used another relay operator in North America, WBCQ in Maine, run by Al Weiner.

LaserRadio.net was one of the names used by London based entrepreneur Andrew Yeates and used a BCM mail drop facility in central London.   The programmes were presented by Julian Clover and Paul Goodwin and included a Media Show for radio enthusiasts. It was run by Geoff Rogers, a well known Radio Jackie DJ, who was also responsible for hosting the online service.

At one stage the name of the project was changed to **Euronet** but the team then joined forces with a Dutch radio entrepreneur called Ruud Poeze with a view to expanding their use of the LASER name and starting a new station in the Netherlands.

Laser 828

In 2003, a UK registered company called **Laser Radio Limited** announced that they had been awarded a network of small low powered AM frequencies in the Netherlands.   They were partnered with a Dutch company called *Quality Radio* who had previously operated stations in Utrecht and other sites in the Netherlands.

"It is very exciting for ourselves and our Dutch partners, said Laser Radio Ltd's MD, Andrew Yeates. "We have some exciting program plans, that we are looking forward to put into practice on AM, which still has a future."

Mr Yeates used the name for some test programmes he was transmitting via Short Wave stations in Eastern Europe. The consortium planned to launch as LASER 828, named after their most powerful licence, near Rotterdam.

The new frequencies awarded to Laser 828 were:

Heinenoord	828 kHz
Echt	1035 kHz
Markerwaard	1224 kHz
Lopik	1395 kHz
Amsterdam	1557 kHz.

The 828 transmitter was for a 20 kilowatts signal just south of Rotterdam which would give an excellent signal over the Netherlands. One can't imagine why the network of transmitters was not brought into use. They expired after 8 years. Laser Radio Limited also produced programmes which were carried by Short Wave transmitters in Latvia and Lithuania.

Laser Radio and Quality Radio were expected to market their new station as **Laser828.** The Dutch branch of Radio Caroline, who broadcast programmes online and via satellite also sought these frequencies, but their applications were refused.

Intellectual Property

The 'Laser Radio' name is an excellent one and many organisations covet such useful names as this. Several companies have been registered using the Laser name and in 2002, a company executive in the UK called Andrew Yeates registered the name **LASER RADIO**.

The protection such patents offers usually lasts for ten years and in 2012 Ray Anderson noticed that it had lapsed. Ray is a serial radio entrepreneur who had previously owned the Communicator and launched Laser Hot Hits. He applied for the name to be registered in his name, was successful and LASER RADIO is now officially in his name, until 2024.

Laser in the Movies

About half a dozen readers of the book about the life of the MV Communicator have contacted me and suggested that it would make a great film. This is not the first time budding scriptwriters have thought that the life on an offshore radio station would transpose very well to the silver screen, or indeed the small screen (TV).

Well known DJs from the 1960s **Paul Burnett**, who sailed on Radio 270, and **Emperor Rosko** who was on Radio Caroline have both written screen plays and touted them around the film companies.

BBC Radio 1 DJ **Mike Read**, although from the next generation along, also tried to solicit interest; his script reads really well and he is an accomplished author.

More recently, former Laser Hot Hits DJ **DL Bogart** wrote a script about life on the ship. Indeed, DL wrote eight screen plays and had six of them accepted, but none have yet made it to general release. (see page 101 for more details)

Former Laser Chief Engineer **Blake Williams** did make it onto celluloid, several times in fact. Since 2006 he has appeared in quite a few movies, many have been on general release and are often seen on TV.

One example of Blake's TV roles is in the modern day western *Longmire*, which stars Robert Taylor and Lou Diamond Phillips. Blake also appears in the movie *Crazy Heart* starring Jeff Bridges, and in *Did You Hear About the Morgans*? alongside Hugh Grant, Sarah Jessica Parker and Mary Steenbergen. So look out for a true Laser star on the big screen and the one eyed monster in your home!

As far as we know, no other Laser team member has made it in the movies yet, although **David Lee Stone** did have aspirations to do so before his death. **Charlie the Seawolf** can be seen quite often on current affairs TV programmes, explaining American politics and the latest Trump story.

In 2009 Richard Curtis directed a British comedy film called *The Boat That Rocked*. It was about a fictitious radio ship in the sixties, called Radio Rock and starred Bill Nighy and Phillip Seymour Hoffman with Rhys Ifans and Kenneth Branagh. The film has now been shown in most countries worldwide but was not an immediate success at the Box Office as had been hoped and lost money for its backers but continues to be shown on major TV channels; ITV scheduled it as their top Saturday Night movie in February 2017.

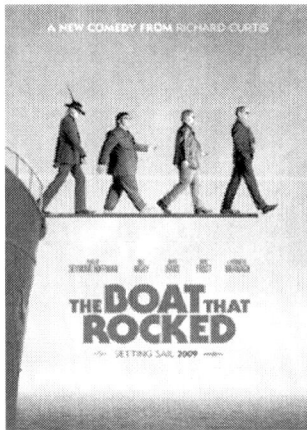

The film (which was called *Pirate Radio* in the USA, *Good Morning England* in France and *Rock Wave* in Russia) was a romantic comedy. Curtis has a long track record for such movies, invariably big hits, such as *4 Weddings and a Funeral*, *Bridget Jones Diary*, *NottingHill* and *Love Actually*. He also directed many TV series including the *Vicar of Dibley* and *Mr Bean.*

Curtis maintains that the film was a fictional comedy and not meant to be a documentary. Some die-hard radio enthusiasts however lambasted its lack of facts and reality but the movie's soundtrack was met with very wide approval.

Some of the equipment in *The Boat That Rocked* were loaned by Radio Caroline and Laser while some Caroline DJs and executives consulted the production company in the making of the film.

Radio Dag in Holland

A key event in the world of offshore radio is staged every year in the Netherlands, called the Radio Dag (Radio Day). For many years these were run by Sir Hans Knot, Martin van der Ven and Rob Olthof. Others have now stepped into run them and in 2017 the event is being held in Harlingen, the home of one of the last remaining offshore radio ships, the lightship *Jenni Baynton*, widely heard as *Radio Seagull.*

Other remaining radio ships are the former Radio Veronica ship the Norderney which is moored in the middle of Amsterdam and often seen on TV hosting music parties. Radio Caroline's last ship, the MV Ross Revenge, is moored on the River Blackwater in Essex and used regularly for broadcasting - you can still visit it, see next section on Radio Caroline.

In 2009 the Dutch Radio Dag had a special Laser panel discussion to celebrate Laser's 25th birthday. Several Laser DJs attended, including Johnny Lewis, Charlie Wolf and Jessie Brandon plus *Laser Hot Hits* owner Ray Anderson and long serving DJ Mike Barrington.

Jessie, Seawolf & Mike at a Radio Dag Laser special

Radio Day, 2017

The *Radio Dag* event in 2017 is being held on Saturday the 20th May in the Dutch harbour town of Harlingen. That's the home of the lightship 'Jenni Baynton', the base of Radio Seagull but the ship often broadcasts as many as three radio stations on its AM transmitters. Laser is scheduled to be a major talking point in 2017 and the day includes a presentation by Paul Rusling whose Laser books will be on sale.

The event is being held in a modernised warehouse "De Entrepot" on the Harlingen dockside. From the quayside a tender will take visitors to visit the Radio Seagull ship. You can witness the station broadcasting, on 747AM, with several well known offshore radio personalities taking part. Admission is €15 with the tender trip to the radio ship costing €10. You can book at these rates via email: *radiodagharlingen@gmail.com.* Maybe we shall see you there? (Anoraks are optional!)

Radio Seagull's lightship Jenni Baynton in Harlingen

Radio Caroline

And finally, what became of Radio Caroline? After Laser left, Radio Caroline was once again alone, and continues today, over twenty years later.

An extension of territorial waters meant she had to sail further out to sea and anchor at a more exposed location. The magnificent 280 feet tall radio tower was lost overboard just after the hurricane of 1987, seriously affecting coverage.

Two years later she was raided by armed thugs who claimed to be acting for the Dutch government. They took or smashed a lot of the equipment but still Radio Caroline bounced back. When the Government assigned the coveted 558AM frequency to local radio, Caroline had to move to a poorer slot along the dial. At the end of 1991 she lost an anchor and was stranded on the notorious Goodwin Sands.

After the crew were rescued by helicopter, the ship was dragged into Dover harbour by tugs and impounded. She was licensed for low power broadcasts and is now anchored on the River Blackwater in Essex. Radio Caroline programmes are usually broadcast from the ship or from studios in Rochester, Kent and heard around the world online and on DAB.

In 2017 it is widely expected that Radio Caroline will be awarded a community radio licence enabling the station to broadcast once again on her spiritual home, the medium wave band.

Radio Caroline is still a free format with her DJs able to choose from a very wide playlist of over 10,000 album tracks. A big contrast to other stations in the UK, some who play as few as 500 different tracks over a month. As well as the traditional Caroline album stream, she also broadcasts an all gold station called *Caroline Flashback* and a weekend station *Caroline North,* rebroadcast by Manx Radio in the Isle of Man .

The Ross Revenge has now had a new mast fitted and a makeover. It continues to be used for programmes and the station now run boat trips to take visitors out and visit the studios where so much radio history took place. They have a shop on board selling all kinds of interesting memorabilia. A piece of radio history and a great day out for all the family!

UK Radio Today

Radio One today is best described as an "alternative new music" station, with hit songs not getting much airplay, even in daytime shows. The station plays a lot of urban contemporary music and 'BritPop' and more new music than almost any other UK station. Radio One doesn't have any disc jockeys, just social commentators and communicators who are claimed to be more in touch with today's youth than the popular DJs of yesteryear, who its controller once dismissed as dinosaurs.

BBC Radio 2 has always targetted a more mature audience and todays incarnation of what many still think of as being the old Light Programme has hired many of the old dinosaurs DJs that Radio One threw out. The station brought its music format up to date that it has been able to absorb pop music fans, most of them were those listeners discarded by Radio One. BBC Radio 2 effectively became an AC (adult contemporary) station most of the time. Its format however is still so loose that most American radio experts would not recognise it as AC!

Variety Quotient

BBC Radio One play around 3,500 unique tracks each month and a total of ten thousand 'plays' of music that one can hear over that period. Sister station Radio 2 plays closer to 5,000 different tracks in a month, which is about two thirds of its monthly total plays.

Expressing those figures as a radio or percentages gives a variety quotient or gauge that indicates how many of the tracks are repeatedly played over and over on a station. The figures for Radio One are 37% at the moment and it's an admirable 65% for Radio 2. The closer the variety quotient gets to 100% the more varied a station's playlist is and the less repetition of music.

Taking the figures of the entire radio industry in the UK together shows 6% variety (28,200 unique tracks and 490,000 total tracks played, although that's probably not a good camparison. Figures are available for most music-led stations.

Local commercial stations on FM tend to play only 1,000 or so different tracks, from a 6,000 total plays per month. This shows a much tighter playlist with not so wide a variety as one would hear on the national BBC channels. The variety quotient for most stations ranges from only 6 to 12%.

Most of the local commercial stations score only around ten to fifteen per cent on a variety gauge that considers the ratio of unique tracks to the total number of plays. i.e. a low variety score is a poor variety of music, with the small library repeated frequently. By contrast BBC Radio One scores 35% and Radio 2 almost twice as high at 65%, which means that it is playing a much wider variety of music, more unique tracks means a bigger record 'library'.

Do most radio listeners prefer less variety or do they actually want a short playlist of songs purely drawn from the latest charts? That is a very pertinent question that managers and programmers must decide. It's an argument which continues to rage in the radio industry.

Extensive research has been carried out in the USA and in many other markets to discover exactly what will attract the radio audience. Do they prefer a short play list with little variety or do listeners get fatigued and want variety?

Radio 2 has the largest audience and the biggest variety of music in British radio, as measured by a variety quotient, which seems to suggest the wide variety of music artistes and genres is more favoured by listeners. It employs a wide range of presenters too, with some being heard daily and some only once a week, or even less.

Listener preferences do vary with different age and demographic groups too; the sophisticated advertiser and his agents will look closely at the spending power of potential listeners. They will also want to know the demographic breakdown of a radio station's audience, which can vary tremendously according to the time or the day. This is one of the reasons why many stations like to homogenise their station's programming, so the listener knows exactly what to expect when he or she tunes in.

Some other factors that affect a radio station's audience size are the signal quality, including its position on the dial, and the lack of direct competition. In the UK the licensing authority have resolutely refused to allow any real competition for sttions on the traditional AM and FM broadcast bands.

This has led to some stations ignoring the kind of research used in other markets and some in the UK radio industry have often scorned research or at least placed little reliance on it. Many stations have simply rejected all research as being "too expensive" or simply unnecessary. Some news for them: not if it's done right it's not!

Training Talent

Few radio station operators and programmers are willing to take a chance on new initiatives or presentation techniques. This is one of the factors that are beginning to stagnate radio output. It is worrying many experienced broadcasters that there are fewer training grounds now for radio presenters.

Since the 1960s, offshore radio has provided a first rate test bed for new radio talent. Many senior radio executives and leading DJs got their break as a radio rookie on offshore radio. Richard Park on Radio Scotland, Tony Blackburn on Radio Caroline, and many more, although some of them seem too shy to acknowledge their roots!

Those ILR stations that broadcast overnight previously tried out new talent on the 'graveyard shifts' but the rush to networking has removed that opening for the would-be DJs. Where can they go now for the much needed for experience?

Some universities offer media courses with modules of radio broadcast training, but a lot are based on text books and anecdotal lectures. This is no substitute for getting experience which can only be done "on the job." Voice coaching and critique sessions can help, but nothing replaces that learning to fly a radio programme by the seat of your pants.

Community radio, hospital and other in-house stations and the online streamers are almost the only place left where radio talent can develop. Where they can make mistakes and build their confidence. The few options now for new entrants are volunteer based, so new entrants must be very committed.

Training of talent is still woefully lacking in the UK. Encouraging egos, developing dynamic thinking and other vital creative methods just isn't being done and it's now seriously diminishing the pool of capable radio personalties.

Constricting what a DJ says stops them learning and using the 'street talk' used by kids today. DJs need to use the strong motivational words that sell. Such powerful words are not only needed in commercials, but in regular dialogue as they are useful to sell the radio station to listeners. Getting a team of DJs to all recite a corny strap line isn't going to increase audience. It's far more likely to chase large chunks of the audience away and the jock too who will become disheartened.

The world is however changing and everyone wants everything immediately, it's the the 'instant gratification' element. Many musicians become stars overnight by way of exposure on TV talent shows such as *The X Factor* and *Britain's Got Talent*. Few singers and musicians have the patience to learn to play instruments properly by slogging for a couple of years around the pub and club circuits to build their name. With several software based apps to vary voice pitch it's not even necessary to sing in tune any more! Is the radio industry heading the same way?

More damage is being done by so many stations being owned by a handful of groups who network many of their programmes. This diminishes the pool of radio talent and makes it increasingly harder to recruit.

Even when a station has its own presenter(s), they often play the same tracks as their sister stations, with playlists being synchronised around their stations in the network. In some areas stations from different areas are audible, but they are invariably playing exactly the same music!

Many people are saddened at the loss of many personalities from radio, and it's not just the personalities themselves. Many people choose the radio for music in preference to their own choice on an iPod for one thing – the presentation. The host becomes much more than a button presser. They are a friend to the listener who relies on them for companionship, for entertainment and for keeping them informed. There are a lot of lonely people out there.

Good radio hosts need nurturing, encouraging, training and given the freedom and space to let their creativity develop. Todays market, despite many radio stations now operating, is becoming so tight and controlled that new talent is being rejected or suppressed.

Today's radio is not letting the new Kenny Everetts, the Noel Edmonds, the Mike Reads, Tony Blackburns or other personalities come to the fore. Their replacements who seem devoid of character, simply recite nonsense from a screen like a parrot. Any trace of humour, personality or individuality is extinguished.

Focus Groups

While some presenters and radio station managers are intimidated by consultants it is clear that radio as a whole needs to be encouraged to help develop creativity. It needs to invest in training its own on air talent and not try and replace them by having the music chosen by focus groups. These are invariably random passers-by with no background in music or idea of the material that attracts radio listeners.

It must surely be pretty pointless when deciding a playlist to ask for the views of people who are not properly motivated. It must be far better to ensure that the station's own presenters understand how to use music to its best effect. Help to boost their creative skills complement and stimulate adventurous programming, not stifle it by limiting vocabulary, topics or the length of each piece of dialogue.

Losing your listeners

Radio works best when unfettered and when it's driven by talent with passion for their area, the music and life. Forcing them to stick to irrelevant phrases from liner cards, play only music chosen by focus groups and then to encapsulate their dialogue so its just staccato or short bursts of meaningless 'clap-trap' will not win the audience a radio station deserves.

The best way to lose your listeners (and probably your team) is to take the steps that some UK stations have recently tried. Gag the talent, remove them from playlist decisions and have them recite strap lines that are irrelevant and quite often laughable. It will simply turn off listeners and totally demoralise staff. Imposing such draconian measures to a radio station says only one thing: if you feel you need to programme like this then you have failed and hired the wrong hosts.

When the variety gauges for stations are compared to audience figures, especially 'time spent listening' it's not so clear that there is universal public preference for more varied stations. BBC Radio 2 attracts most listeners but not the most 'time spent listening.' It has the oldest 'heritage' of all stations now broadcasting and is the direct descendent of the Light Programme which began in the 1940s.

It also has the best transmission network and is more universally available, being audible on several frequencies in most areas. Radio 2 also has extensive resources, with the BBC's network of local stations feeding material in to it.

The ILR stations have tried to shake off the 'local' tag and are becoming quasi-national, as the licensing shackles prohibiting networking are loosened. This is a trend that may well continue as in early 2017 the UK Government invited comments from stations and the public on changes.

Should radio stations continue to have only formats mandated by their licensing authority or should they be permitted to vary the genres of music they play? That's just one of the questions being asked now of stations and others .

If the ties on programme formats are released, perhaps we shall see an unseemly rush to just one lowest common denominator format, or shall we get a genuine broadening of programming and listener choice?

Rank	Top Radio Formats for Highest Proportion of Listeners Going to Radio Website	Where the Bulk of Listeners Are by Age Cell		
		18-34	35-55	55+
1	Modern Rock/New Rock	62.7%	34.4%	2.8%
2	Adult Alternative	33.9%	55.6%	10.5%
3	Sports	24.5%	48.6%	26.9%
4	Rock (50% Current 50% Old)	49.4%	45.6%	5.0%
5	Jazz	17.6%	46.9%	35.5%
6	Talk	15.4%	44.6%	40.0%
7	Public Radio	19.1%	45.4%	35.4%
8	Classic Rock	26.9%	62.7%	10.3%
9	Classical	15.4%	43.4%	41.1%
10	CHR	63.9%	32.0%	4.1%
11	Modern AC	42.8%	50.7%	6.5%
12	News/Talk	14.2%	42.6%	43.2%
13	Hot AC	41.2%	51.1%	7.7%
14	Dance CHR	70.6%	25.9%	3.5%
15	Contemporary Christian	27.9%	56.1%	16.0%
	% of the total adult population	30.7%	39.7%	29.6%

How to Read: 62.7% of Modern Rock/New Rock Adult Listeners are between the ages of 18 and 34

More new stations ?

It has long been my belief that the biggest sin perpetrated by the licensing authorities on the public has been the refusal to grant new licences for different types of radio stations. The appearance of Laser and the resulting reorganisation that led to radio being removed from the IBA and put with a new Radio Authority gave hope that at last there would be changes. There were indeed changes, but the same old brigade of establishment figures were put in charge, often former military men who are hardly the best equipped leaders for change in such an important medium. Certainly not for the entertainment parts of it.

My personal hope was that we would have enjoyed a proliferation of radio stations with no artificial barrier to the type of programme format or choice of content, other than the standard requirement that content always be honest, legal, decent and truthful. Sadly, some of those basic criteria have now gone by the board with vulgarity, profanity and the most appalling language being used at times. Perhaps this is partly the result of DJs not being trained on overnight shifts?

Once again there is hope that the latest regulator, OFCOM, will open the gates a lot wider and let us have more stations, with more formats and their ownership in far more hands. They should be free to operate commercially and not have their hands tied behind their backs, which is being done in order to protect a few commercial monopolies.

Will brave-hearted radio entrepreneurs be allowed to open new stations for small, niche markets, perhaps attracting more listeners to radio? That was certainly the effect when the Radio Authority began to license new stations in the 1990s. Jazz, country, black music, Asian, and easy listening stations were all added to the dial, albeit only in the large urban areas. National stations added three specialist formats of classical music, rock music and talk.

Or will any new stations be blocked by the mega-size conglomerates that now run most stations, with their bleating cries of "they are stealing our listeners", probably the most short-sighted and protectionist stance they could take.

The spirit of Laser was always "the more radio stations, the merrier." It was almost a mantra and manifested with very unusual please from the station to advertisers. Fillers were broadcast frequently, extolling the virtues and advantages of advertising on the radio. They always suggested that prospective advertisers should call their local radio station, but if their business was international their sales team should call Laser.

Other questions in the consultation cover the locaton of studios. Until now radio stations have been compelled to originate programmes in their target area with few exceptions. The commercial stations must also observe strict rules preventing centralising news gathering. While these are sensible in principle, in practice it is surely wasteful and somewhat extravagant to have a newsroom manned around the clock in an area where there are unlikely to be breaking stories.

Where new extra local stations have been permitted the authorities have imposed quite draconian and restrictive programming rules, relating to the amount of various types of music that can be played. Rival stations have employed monitors to listen in to rival stations, compile playlists from their output and any discrepancies reported back to the licensing authority. It's a 'dog eat dog' world is ILR!

Financial penalties are imposed by OFCOM (the licensing authority) where a station is proved to be deviating from its alloted music genre and could even result in loss of a licence. All for playing the wrong kind of music! There have been many intense arguments over what type of genre various artists and even their different songs fall into. This can hardly be a healthy environment in which radio can flourish!

Is the big problem for radio in the UK similar to that the whole world over, where the cult of the personality DJ has been all but killed off? Was it killed off by accountants, or is this just a natural evolution of radio? Many of the world's finest DJs have their own views, but are afraid to express their thoughts lest it destroys any future possibility of any radio work.

One who isn't too concerned about getting a full time job in radio is former Caroline and Luxembourg personality DJ, Tony Prince. He has produced a series of mini programmes which track the cult of the DJ, most are available on YouTube. His introduction to the latest eposide was very relevant to today's radio DJ scenario:

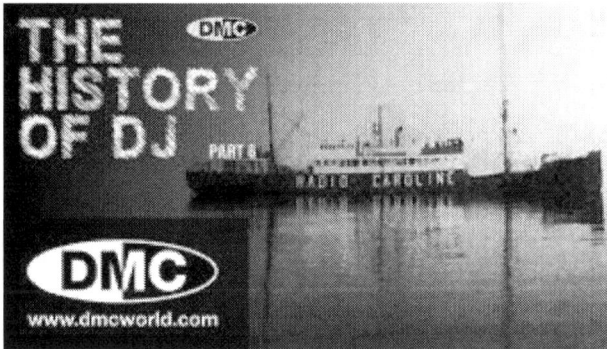

"The History of DJ has arrived at a point in time where the character of the individual DJ has been extracted from the airwaves of the world. With tight playlists and strict on-air control, the majority of radio DJs find themselves in a straight-jacket, with Spotify, Shazam, Mixcloud, Soundcloud and almost every record that was ever made into a video now available on YouTube at the press of a button.

The final frontier for radio listening is mainly in the car or, if you have SKY, on the TV menu bar. The day is long gone when kids listened beneath their pillow with a transistor radio and an earpiece to hide their nocturnal love for listening to their favourite DJ from their parents.

A flurry of internet radio channels, blogs and pirate radio operators try to compete in a world where most DJ broadcasters work for love not money. At best local FM radio stations pay some sort of wages but, in their competitive arena, they can't pay what they don't have.

"Fortunately however, DJs and wannabe DJs are prepared to work for very little," says Tony. "It is this fire in the belly of the DJs and their passion for music that keeps radio alive."

Legendary music phenomenom Stevie Wonder has also ackowledged that "many DJs are bigger stars than the musicians they play." In a plea to the music industry in 2017 he claims that the mushrooming number of copyright collectors is hurting small stations, such as the one he owns in Los Angeles. KJLH is a 'urban contemporary' formatted station that also uses the identification 'Free Radio' as Stevie gives his DJs a free hand in music selection.

The latest RAJAR figures show that more people than ever are now listening to radio. Many broadcasters, even the BBC, are cutting costs by ditching live DJs at times. While not suicidal, this certainly sounds like they are self-harming. Do listeners really just want a stream of non stop music or do they want personalities hosting programmes?

With the UK authorities now consulting all interested parties on which way radio should develop, perhaps we might finally see an expansion in the number of licenses available?

There is capacity on AM, FM and DAB mutiplexes for new radio stations; do YOU have an idea for a format that you believe could be commercially successful? Perhaps it's time for the DJs to take control of radio stations and back their programming convinctions with their money? Its now easier than ever to launch a radio station and I know just the team of experts to help you do it!

Message from the Author

I hope this book has answered many of the questions you might have had about the operation of Laser. I tried to explain how the industry's failings and shortcomings made it so easy to build that large audience, why Laser was launched, and why a radio project owned by an Irishman and put together by three Englishmen, hired only American DJs.

Laser's failure to exploit its huge audience can only be attributed to the ineptitude of the sales team. It's nigh on unbelievable that the lucrative airtime deals that had been negotiated before the station launched were never completed.

The way that the small and under-resourced team were able to continue broadcasts for as long as they did was due to the team's diligence and hard work. They all deserve some kind of medal. Many of the team who set up and ran Laser are available for work on new projects. Contact me at the email below for details

Paul Rusling

EMail: paul@worldofradio.co.uk

Many souvenirs of Laser are available

on the World of Radio web site (*worldofradio.co.uk*)

APPENDICES

Internet Links of Interest

World of Radio .... www.worldofradio.co.uk

Worldwide Broadcast Consultants ... www.worldwidebroadcast.co

Offshore Radio Guide .... www.offshore-radio.de

Pirate Radio Hall of Fame .... www.offshoreradio.co.uk

Hans Knot International report .... www.hansknot.com

Offshore Echoes Magazine .... www.offshoreechos.com

Pirate Radio Memories .... http://www.piratememories.com

Radio Caroline .... www.radiocaroline.co.uk

Radio Seagull .... http://radioseagull.com

Laser Tribute station .... http://www.alleuroperadio.com

Bob Le-Roi .... www.bobleroi.co.uk

Wireless Waffler .... https://wirelesswaffle.wordpress.com

LASER 558

Official Announcement of Laser's birth & Format.

PRESS

NEW OFFSHORE RADIO STATION AIRS CONTINUOUS HIT MUSIC

Hit music fans throughout Western Europe now have a new radio station.
LASER 558 All Europe Radio is transmitting from aboard the M. V.
Communicator anchored in international waters in the North Sea.

LASER 558 broadcasts a 25,000 watt signal at 558khz A.M. (538 metres
medium wave) promising listeners they'll never be more than a minute
away from music.

Deejay personalities from the United States play a long list of hit
records, blending new releases with established hits and classics
from Europe, Scandinavia and the United States. There are brief news
headlines once an hour with no commentaries or political announcements.

"Unlike the pirate stations of the past, LASER 558 is a legal radio
station," says Roy Lindau, President of Music Media International,
exclusive worldwide sales representatives of the station. "Since the
ship is registered outside of Europe, transmits from international
waters, is owned and operated by a Panamanian corporation and staffed
and supplied by citizens of the United States, the station is, in the
opinion of counsel, entirely legal."

Multinational advertisers based outside the signatory states of the
European Convention can place advertising schedules on the station
through MMI's New York office at 341 Madison Avenue. Rates are low
compared with most commercial radio in Europe. Thirty second commercial
advertisements range from $40 to $250 depending on the time of day.

Using brand new transmitters and a highly efficient antenna system, the
station will broadcast a signal covering more than 164 million people
over 15 years of age in nine countries. Lindau is projecting an early
audience of 10 million weekly.

MUSIC MEDIA INTERNATIONAL
341 Madison Avenue · New York, N.Y. 10017 U.S.A.

Operations Manual

This is the original programme instructions to Laser staff on board the radio ship, containing:

Music Scheduling

Hot Clock,

Format Notes,

DJ Shifts,

Special Duties,

Logging commercials shorthand,

Laser IDs,

Laser Music Promo trailers,

Laser Fillers and Strap Lines,

Rules for Direct Marketing commercials,

Laser Broadcast Standards.

NOTE. These are copies of the original well-thumbed binder, used on the ship by most of the on air staff. Tri-hole punched and bound (US style) it has some hole marks and other blemishes visible, was produced on the MMI office typewriter and the paper is now 33 years old!

LASER 558

ALL EUROPE RADIO

OPERATIONS MANUAL

LASER 558   ALL EUROPE RADIO   OPERATIONS MANUAL

L A S E R

ALL EUROPE RADIO

OPERATIONS MANUAL

CONTENTS

LASER 558   ALL EUROPE RADIO   OPERATIONS MANUAL

LASER 558
ALL EUROPE RADIO
MUSIC FORMAT

LASER 558 PROGRAMS ALL MUSIC ALL THE TIME.   DEEJAY PERSONALITIES
PLAY A LONG LIST OF HIT RECORDS, BLENDING NEW RELEASES WITH
ESTABLISHED   HITS   AND   CLASSICS   FROM   THE   UK,   THE   CONTINENT,
SCANDINAVIA AND THE U.S.

THE   ACCENT   IS ON THE   MUSIC.   MORE   MUSIC,   LESS   TALK.   NEWS
HEADLINES   AIR   ON   THE   HOUR.   NO   POLITICAL   ANNOUNCEMENTS   OR
COMMENTARIES.   COMMERCIAL   ANNOUNCEMENTS   ARE   LIMITED   TO   SIX
MINUTES AN HOUR WITH NO BREAK LONGER THAN A MINUTE.   THE STATION
IS   PRESENTED   IN   ENGLISH WITH MULTI-LINGUAL   STATION   ID'S   AND
MUSIC.

DEEJAYS   MAINTAIN   AN UPBEAT TEMPO WITH THEIR SELECTION OF   MUSIC
AND   COMMENTS.   OVERALL STATION SOUND IS BASED ON A 'HOT   CLOCK'
THAT FEATURES 15 TO 16 RECORDS IN THE HOUR.   EACH HOUR INCLUDES A
MIXTURE   OF   CURRENT   AND   RECURRENT   HITS,   ETHNIC   MUSIC,   NEW
RELEASES, AND OLDIES FROM BEFORE 1980.

        SAMPLE ARTISTS FROM   MARCH 1984:
              ---CURRENT---
              CULTURE CLUB
              PAUL YOUNG
              DURAN DURAN
              EURYTHMICS
              BIG COUNTRY
              JOHN LENNON
              YES
              MADNESS
              THE ALARM

              ---ETHNIC---
              MICHAEL JACKSON
              UB40
              LIONEL RITCHIE
              TINA TURNER
              GLORIA GAYNOR
              MUSICAL YOUTH

            ---NEW RELEASES---
              CYNDI LAUPER
              MATHEW WILDER
              JOE FAGIN
              NENA

          ---OLDIES---
              THE BYRDS
              BEATLES
              ROLLING STONES
              THE KINKS
              THE SUPREMES
              SPENCER DAVIS GROUP

LASER 558   ALL EUROPE RADIO   OPERATIONS MANUAL

```
        L A S E R   558

      ALL EUROPE RADIO

        MUSIC FORMAT

        HOT CLOCK


  H = HITS         6 PER HOUR

  N = NEW          1 PER HOUR

  R = RECURRENT    2 PER HOUR

  E = ETHNIC*      3 PER HOUR


  080+ = OLDIES 1980+      1 PER HOUR

  073+ = OLDIES '73-'80    1 PER HOUR

  OP73 = OLDIES PRE '73    1 PER HOUR+


  * = MOTOWN, REGGAE, URBAN CONTEMPORARY
```

NEWS

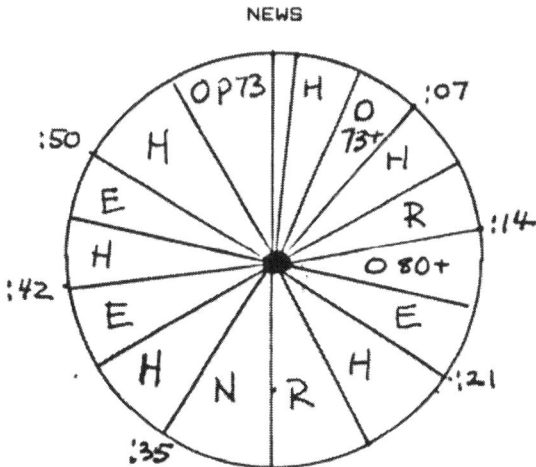

LASER 558   ALL EUROPE RADIO   OPERATIONS MANUA

L A S E R   558

ALL   EUROPE   RADIO

FORMAT NOTES

TIME CHECKS
    1.   AT LEAST SIX TIMES PER HOUR; AT TOP OF HOUR;
        30 MINUTES PAST AND FOUR OTHER TIMES ADLIB.

    2.   GIVE GMT FIRST, THEN CONTINENTAL TIME; ALWAYS
        SAY "IT'S _____ MINUTES PAST (ACTUAL HOUR)."

WEATHER
    1.   DON'T DO WEATHERCASTS AT ALLL.

    2.   ONLY EXCEPTION; MAJOR STORMS WIDE AREA.

NEWS
    1.   UP TO 60 SECONDS ON THE HOUR ONLY.

    2.   0500 IS 1ST NEWS OF DAY; 2200, LAST.

    3.   MUST BE ABSOLUTELY APOLITICAL.

    4.   AVOID BRITISH SLANT. CONCENTRATE ON INTERNATIONAL
        HEADLINES WITH DATELINES ACROSS EUROPE AND AROUND
        THE WORLD. DON'T MENTION ITEMS LIKE 'ROYAL NAVY',
        'ROYAL COMMISSION', ETC., FOR THERE ARE MANY
        MONARCHIES IN OUR COVERAGE AREA.

    5.   IF YOU CAN'T WRITE A HEADLINE THAT SOUNDS
        APOLITICAL, CUT THE STORY ALTOGETHER.

    6.   DEEJAYS SHOULD READ FIRST NEWSCAST IN THEIR
        SHIFT. THEREAFTER NEWSCASTS SHOULD BE PREPARED
        AND READ BY DEEJAY FOR NEXT SHIFT.

COMMERCIALS
    1.   NO BREAKS LONGER THAN A MINUTE.

    2.   SIX BREAKS AN HOUR.

    3.   NO SPOTS LONGER THANN 60 SECONDS.

    4.   TWO 30'S MAY RUN BACK TO BACK IN SAME BREAK.

PROMOS, FILLERS AND ID'S

    1.   THE FILLERS SHOULD BE READ LIVE ON A
        ROTATING BASIS. DON'T VARY WORDING.

    2.   LIVE PROMOS SHOULD RUN IN EVERY SHIFT FOR THE
        SATURDAY NIGHT DANCE PARTY & THE SIXTIES SUNDAY.

3.   PRODUCED PROMOS (LASER EFX) SHOULD RUN AT LEAST
      TWICE PER HOUR. NEW RECORD PROMO SHOULD BE
      PRODUCED EVERY TWO WEEKS.

4.   FOREIGN LANGUAGE ID'S SHOULD RUN ONCE PER HOUR.

5.   ALL OF THE ABOVE SHOULD BE SCHEDULED ALONG
      WITH COMMERCIALS AND DIRECT MARKETING SPOTS TO
      GIVE EVERY HOUR A COMMERCIAL FEELING.   THIS
      STATION SHOULD NOT SOUND COMMERCIAL FREE AT
      ANY TIME.

LASER 558   ALL EUROPE RADIO   OPERATIONS MANUAL

L A S E R   558

ALL EUROPE RADIO

FORMAT NOTES

SATURDAY NIGHT DANCE PARTY

    1.   RUNS SAT 2200 TO SUN 0200.

    2.   FREE - WHEELING DANCE CUTS WITH FEW INTERRUPTIONS.
        NO NEWS. COMMERCIALS LIMITED TO SPONSORSHIP BILLBOARD
        ANNOUNCEMENTS.

SIXTIES SUNDAY

    1.   RUNS RUN 0600 TO 2200.

    2.   PLAY TO OLDER AUDIENCE USING NOSTALGIC APPEALS.

LASER 558   ALL EUROPE RADIO   OPERATIONS MANUAL

```
        L A S E R   558

    ALL EUROPE RADIO

    DEEJAY SHIFTS


    REGULAR SCHEDULE
    (4 HR SHIFTS)

0500-0900        RIC HARRIS OR BUZZ CODY

0900-1300        DAVID LEE STONE

1300-1700        BUZZ CODY OR  MIGHTY JOE YOUNG

1700-2100        JESSIE BRANDON OR MELINDA BOND

2100-0100        MELINDA BOND

0100-0300        BLAKE WILLIAMS OR MIGHTY JOE YOUNG

SHORE   LEAVE    ---------------------------------
```

LASER 558   ALL EUROPE RADIO   OPERATIONS MANUAL

L A S E R 558

DEEJAY PERSONALITY LINE-UP

LASER Deejays are all native born Americans with impressive
credentials as experienced professional broadcasters.

DAVID LEE STONE hails from California where he worked as a
deejay, program director, actor, model and lead singer with
a rock group in Los Angeles.

STEVE MASTERS was attracted to radio while attending college
in Boston. When he graduated he landed a deejay shift at one
of the major Boston stations where he was later discovered by
LASER.

MELINDA BOND is from New Haven, Connecticut and began her
radio career at Yale. Before joining LASER, she was a deejay
at a major New Haven station.

RIC HARRIS is from New York and became hooked on radio while
working toward a degree in Mathematics. He joins LASER from a
station on Cape Cod where he was a deejay and producer.

CAPTAIN "BUZZ" CODY joined LASER from Detroit where he became
a deejay after serving with the Marines in Vietnam.

JESSIE BRANDON studied broadcasting and film production in
Maryland. After graduating with honors, she became a news
reporter for a radio station in Washington, D.C. and quickly
moved on to deejay and music director positions in Hartford,
San Jose and Seattle.

BLAKE WILLIAMS started his own pirate radio station in his
Arizona home when he was only 16! After his formal education
he went "legit" and worked as an Engineer, Producer, Deejay at
several Tucson stations. Blake is also Chief Engineer of LASER.

MIGHTY JOE YOUNG spent the last 12 years at South Florida radio
stations as a deejay, program director prior to joining LASER.
Joe is also Operations Manager of the station.

LASER 558   ALL EUROPE RADIO   OPERATIONS MANUAL

```
              L A S E R   558

           ALL EUROPE RADIO

        DEEJAY SPECIALTIES
```

OPERATIONS MANAGER	MIGHTY JOE YOUNG
MUSIC LIBRARIAN	JESSIE BRANDON
COMPUTER OPERATIONS	DAVID LEE STONE
CHIEF ENGINEER	BLAKE WILLIAMS
PRODUCTION COORDINATOR	RIC HARRIS
FITNESS AND RECREATION	STEVE MASTERS
NEWS COORDINATOR	MELINDA BOND
FORMAT MONITOR	CAPTAIN BUZZ CODY

LASER 558   ALL EUROPE RADIO   OPERATIONS MANUAL

LASER   558

ALL   EUROPE   RADIO

DUTIES OF OPERATIONS MANAGER

1)   MAINTAIN FORMAT

2)   MAINTAIN COMMERCIAL LOG VIA SATELLITE

3)   LOG IN COMMERCIAL MATERIAL

4)   SUPERVISE WORK AND SHIFT SCHEDULES

5)   ACT AS LIASION WITH CAPTAIN AND CREW

6)   MAINTAIN STUDIO CONDITIONS

7)   RUN A WEEKLY STAFF MEETING

LASER 558   ALL EUROPE RADIO   OPERATIONS MANUAL

L A S E R

ALL EUROPE RADIO

COMMERCIAL LOGGING SYSTEM

ONLY COMMERCIAL MATERIAL WILL APPEAR ON THE OFFICIAL LOG.   THERE
ARE SIX COMMERCIAL POSITIONS EACH HOUR WITH A MIXIMUM OF TWO
THIRTY SECOND SPOTS IN EACH POSITION.

BECAUSE OF LOGGING DONE BY TELEX, A SHORTHAND SYSTEM WILL BE
NECESSARY.   EACH HOUR WILL BE IDENTIFIED ON A 24 HOUR BASIS
(GMT).   EACH   COMMMERCIAL POSITION WILL BE IDENTIFIED   AS
:07;:14;:21;:35;:42, OR :50.   NOTE: TWO THIRTY SECOND SPOTS MAY
OCCASIONALLY BE SCHEDULED IN THE SAME POSITION (AD LIB SLOTS
EITHER 1 OR 2).   THESE WILL BE SCHEDULED IN ANY ONE HOUR IN THIS
PRIORITY: 07,35,14,42,21,50.

EXAMPLES:

1.   ONE THIRTY SECOND SPOT IN SECOND PRIORITY FOR 11 TO 12 PM ON
MONDAY WILL RUN AT "MON 2335".

2.   ONE SIXTY SECOND SPOT IN THE SIXTH PRIORITY BETWEEN 7 AND 8AM
ON THURSDAY WILL BE DESIGNATED "THU 0750".

BLANK LOG SHEETS ARE IN SUPPLY.   PLEASE USE GREASE PENCIL AND
PLASTIC SHEETS FOR EACH DAYS LOG.

WE WILL TELEX EACH DAYS LOG 24 HOURS IN ADVANCE. ONLY SOLD
POSITIONS WILL BE TRANSMITTED SO IF A TRANSMISSION LOOKS LIKE
THIS:
         MON   0707   1   AIR FLORIDA   CART AF1
         MON   0735   4   AC DELCO   CART ACD2
         MON   0807   1   FORD   CART F4
         MON   0835   4   DHL   LIVE DHL2

ASSUME THE OTHER SLOTS ARE UNSOLD IN THOSE HOURS AND PLAY MORE
MUSIC.

ALL DISCREPANCIES MUST BE NOTED AND TELEXED BACK TO NEW YORK
(MAKE SURE TELEX IS ACKNOWLEDGED BEFORE DISCARDING YOUR COPY).

EXAMPLE:
DISCREPANCY REPORT   4/25/84

WED 1107 2 MISSED AND RE-SCHEDULED WED. 1207
WED 1307 1 MISSED NOT RE-SCHEDULED

NO OTHER DISCREPANCIES.

ALL SPOTS NOT RUNNING IN THE HOUR ORDERED MUST BE REPORTED IN THE
ABOVE MANNER AS DISCREPANCIES. NO EXCEPTIONS. ALL COMMERCIAL
CARTS WILL BE NUMBERED. LIVE COPY WILL ALSO BE NUMBERED AND KEPT
IN A 3 RING BINDER BOOK IN THE ON-AIR STUDIO.

LASER 558   ALL EUROPE RADIO   OPERATIONS MANUAL

```
                L A S E R    I D'S

                (to be read live)

You're listening to LASER 558...where the hits keep coming!

                -0-

You're listening to LASER 558...where music is never more than
a minute away!

                -0-

You're listening to LASER 558...home of the hits!

                -0-

You're listening to LASER 558...All hits!  All the time!

                -0-

You're listening to All Hit Radio:  Laser 558!

                -0-

You're listening to LASER 558 - All Europe Radio!

                -0-
```

LASER 558   ALL EUROPE RADIO   OPERATIONS MANUAL

L A S E R   M U S I C   P R O M O

(To be produced at least every 2 weeks)

(LASER EFX)

You're listening to Laser All Europe Radio where the hits keep coming.

(LASER EFX)

(Segue to 1st new hit record sample of 4 to 8 bars)

(LASER EFX)

(Segue to 2nd new hit record sample of 4 to 8 bars)

(LASER EFX)

(Segue to 3rd new hit record sample of 4 to 8 bars)

(LASER EFX)

You'll hear these hit records and more -- all this week -- along with the top hits and oldies on LASER 558, where music is never more than a minute away.

(LASER EFX)

LASER 558   ALL EUROPE RADIO   OPERATIONS MANUAL

L A S E R   F I L L E R S

(to be read live)

You're listening to Laser All Europe Radio broadcasting at 558 kilohertz a.m. or a wavelength of 538 metres on medium wave. We're transmitting from aboard the M.V. Communicator in the North Sea. The air waves are free: that's what we believe. And that means we're free to play as much music as we can. The top hits you want to hear. So set your radios at 558 kilohertz or 538 metres and you'll get at least 54 minutes of music every hour. We have no breaks longer than a minute with brief news headlines on the hour to keep you in touch with the world. Let me know what you think about Laser All Europe Radio. Write to me, _____ in care of the 'M. V. Communicator, Post Office Box 1892, Grand Central Station, New York City 10163, U.S.A. I promise to answer as many as I can.

LASER 558   ALL EUROPE RADIO   OPERATIONS MANUAL

L A S E R   F I L L E R S

(to be read live)

Do you have a Laser 558 button on your car radio?   Well, if you don't, here's how you can make one:

First   make sure the first button on your car radio is set at 558 kilohertz A.M. or 538 metres on the medium wave band.   Then   put your finger under the first button.   Lift up and pull the button out towards you.   When you feel a click the button is set.   Now push the button all the way in.   Then what do you have?   A Laser button.   Right there on the first spot on your radio dial.

-0-

When you get into your car, what's the second thing you turn on? The radio, of course.   Millions and millions of cars are out there with radios.   When you get out of the car what's the last thing you turn off?   The radio!   And there's somebody's message in your ears.   You can bet on that.   Now, advertisers: you've got this message in your ears.   To get in touch with millions of drivers throughout Europe, get in touch with radio.   Radio advertising works!

LASER 558   ALL EUROPE RADIO   OPERATIONS MANUAL

L A S E R   F I L L E R S

(to be read live)

What are you doing right now? Driving? Typing? Cooking?
Washing? Chances are you're doing something besides just
listening to the radio. That's what's great about radio.
It's your constant companion — with you wherever you go —
what ever you're doing. Radio messages reach people any
time, anywhere. Now advertisers you've got this
message: If you want to reach people wherever they go,
try radio.
Radio Advertising Works!

LASER 558   ALL EUROPE RADIO   OPERATIONS MANUAL

L A S E R   F I L L E R S

(to be read live)

Did you know that one word can be worth about a thousand pictures? Think about it. Words and sounds can bring out strong images in your mind, while pictures may get in the way. By combining the right words and sounds advertisers can save the cost of thousands of pictures. That's just what radio is all about. More impact fpr less money. Radio advertising works!

-0-

You know ears are marvelous. A radio message goes into the ears and then directly to the computer in your head. Immediately the computer sends a message to the hands to take out some money and buy the merchandise the ears just heard about. Radio advertising works!

LASER 558   ALL EUROPE RADIO   OPERATIONS MANUAL

(ALL 3 SPOTS TO RUN IN SAME HALF HOUR.   THIS RUNS FIRST)

   TEE SHIRT SPOT #1 (LIVE)

EVERY RADIO STATION SHOULD HAVE A TEE-SHIRT FOR ITS LISTENERS AND
IN THE NEXT HALF HOUR, BETWEEN RECORDS, I'M GOING TO TELL YOU HOW
YOU CAN   GET ONE.   WEAR THIS TEE SHIRT AND YOU'LL INSTANTLY BE
IDENTIFIED AS A TRUE SUPPORTER OF FREE COMMUNICATION, FREE RADIO
AND EVERYTHING THAT LASER STANDS FOR. HOW CAN THIS BE?
WELL, IF YOU'VE BEEN LISTENING AWHILE YOU KNOW WE'RE BROADCASTING
FROM THE THE NORTH SEA FROM A SHIP NAMED THE COMMUNICATOR, SO
WE'VE COME UP WITH A COMMUNICATOR TEE SHIRT.IT'S A WHITE
TEE SHIRT WITH A BIG BOLD INTERNATIONAL SIGNAL FLAG ON THE
FRONT.   NO LETTERS. NO NUMBERS. JUST THE FLAG.
THE INTERNATIONAL SIGNAL FLAG USED AT SEA WHICH MEANS
"I WANT TO COMMUNICATE WITH YOU" WHICH IS JUST WHAT THIS
STATION IS ALL ABOUT.   STAY TUNED, AFTER I PLAY SOME MORE MUSIC
I'LL TELL YOU HOW TO ORDER YOUR OWN COMMUNICATOR TEE SHIRT.

LASER 558   ALL EUROPE RADIO   OPERATIONS MANUAL

(ALL 3 SPOTS TO RUN IN SAME HALF HOUR.   THIS RUNS FIRST)

TEE SHIRT SPOT #1 (LIVE)

EVERY RADIO STATION SHOULD HAVE A TEE-SHIRT FOR ITS LISTENERS AND
IN THE NEXT HALF HOUR, BETWEEN RECORDS, I'M GOING TO TELL YOU HOW
YOU CAN   GET ONE.   WEAR THIS TEE SHIRT AND YOU'LL INSTANTLY   BE
IDENTIFIED AS A TRUE SUPPORTER OF FREE COMMUNICATION,   FREE RADIO
AND   EVERYTHING   THAT LASER STANDS FOR.   HOW   CAN THIS   BE?
WELL, IF YOU'VE BEEN LISTENING AWHILE YOU KNOW WE'RE BROADCASTING
FROM   THE   THE NORTH SEA FROM A SHIP NAMED THE   COMMUNICATOR,   SO
WE'VE COME   UP WITH A COMMUNICATOR TEE SHIRT. IT'S A WHITE
TEE SHIRT WITH A BIG BOLD   INTERNATIONAL   SIGNAL FLAG   ON THE
FRONT.   NO LETTERS.   NO NUMBERS.   JUST   THE FLAG.
THE INTERNATIONAL SIGNAL FLAG USED AT SEA   WHICH MEANS
"I WANT TO COMMUNICATE WITH YOU" WHICH IS JUST   WHAT   THIS
STATION IS ALL ABOUT.   STAY TUNED,   AFTER I PLAY SOME MORE MUSIC
I'LL TELL YOU HOW TO ORDER YOUR OWN COMMUNICATOR TEE SHIRT.

LASER 558   ALL EUROPE RADIO   OPERATIONS MANUAL

(ALL 3 SPOTS TO RUN IN SAME HALF HOUR. THIS RUNS SECOND)

TEE SHIRT SPOT #2 (LIVE)

A FEW MOMENTS AGO I WAS TELLING YOU ABOUT OUR COMMUNICATOR TEE
SHIRTS.   IF YOU'VE SEEN ANY OF THE PRESS ABOUT LASER, THESE
ARE THE TEE SHIRTS WORN BY THE OTHER DEEJAYS AND ME IN MOST OF
THE PICTURES,   THEY'RE WHITE TEE SHIRTS WITH A BIG BOLD SIGNAL
FLAG ON THE FRONT. NO LETTERS. NO NUMBERS. JUST THE FLAG.
THE INTERNATIONAL SIGNAL FLAG USED AT SEA WHICH MEANS
"I WANT TO COMMUNICATE WITH YOU" WHICH IS JUST WHAT THIS
STATION IS ALL ABOUT. IF YOU WANT TO SUPPORT FREE
COMMUNICATION AND FREE RADIO LIKE LASER, ORDER YOUR OWN
"COMMUNICATOR" TEE SHIRT TODAY. SEND YOUR NAME AND ADDRESS ALONG
WITH A BANKERS DRAFT OR CASHIERS CHECK FOR THE EQUIVALENT OF
SIX POUNDS STERLING, MADE OUT TO MUSIC MEDIA INTERNATIONAL.
A BANKERS DRAFT OR A CASHIERS CHECK CAN BE PURCHASED AT ANY BANK.
DO NOT SEND PERSONAL CHECKS, MONEY ORDERS OR TRAVELERS CHECKS;
BECAUSE OF LONG COLLECTION DELAYS, THESE CAN NOT BE ACCEPTED.
SEND YOUR BANKERS DRAFT TO;

        MUSIC MEDIA INTERNATIONAL
        341 MADISON AVENUE
        NEW YORK, NY 10017 USA

ALLOW FOUR-SIX WEEKS FOR DELIVERY AND SAY WHETHER YOU WANT
SMALL, MEDIUM, LARGE OR EXTRA LARGE. THAT'S 6 POUNDS STERLING TO;

        MUSIC MEDIA INTERNATIONAL
        341 MADISON AVE.
        NEW YORK, NY 10017 USA

ORDER YOUR COMMUNICATOR TEE SHIRT TODAY!

LASER 558   ALL EUROPE RADIO   OPERATIONS MANUAL

(ALL 3 SPOTS TO RUN IN SAME HALF HOUR THIS RUNS 3RD)

TEE SHIRT SPOT #3

HERE'S MORE INFORMATION ABOUT THOSE COMMUNICATOR TEE SHIRTS

I'VE BEEN TELLING YOU ABOUT. THE ONES WITH THE BIG BOLD SIGNAL

FLAG ON THE FRONT. THE INTERNATIONAL SIGNAL FLAG USED AT SEA

WHICH MEANS "I WANT TO COMMUNICATE WITH YOU". IF YOU WANT TO

SUPPORT FREE COMMUNICATION, FREE RADIO LIKE LASER, ORDER YOUR

"COMMUNICATOR" TEE SHIRT TODAY. SEND YOUR NAME AND ADDRESS

ALONG WITH A BANKERS DRAFT OR CASHIERS CHECK FOR SIX POUNDS

STERLING MADE OUT TO MUSIC MEDIA INTERNATIONAL. A BANKERS

DRAFT OR CASHIERS CHECK CAN BE PURCHASED AT ANY BANK. DO

NOT SEND PERSONAL CHECKS, MONEY ORDERS OR TRAVELERS CHECKS;

BECAUSE OF LONG COLLECTION DELAYS THESE CANNOT BE ACCEPTED.

SEND YOUR CHECK TO; MUSIC MEDIA INTERNATIONAL
                     341 MADISON AVENUE
                     NEW YORK, NY 10017 USA

ALLOW 4 WEEKS FOR DELIVERY AND SAY WHETHER YOU WANT SMALL,

MEDIUM, LARGE OR EXTRA LARGE.

THESE ARE QUALITY TEE SHIRTS. THE DESIGN IS DYED ON THE

FABRIC AND WILL NOT FADE. THAT'S ONLY 6 POUNDS STERLING TO:

          MUSIC MEDIA INTERNATIONAL
          341 MADISON AVENUE
          NEW YORK, NY 10017 USA

ORDER YOUR COMMUNICATOR TEE SHIRT TODAY!

LASER 558   ALL EUROPE RADIO   OPERATIONS MANUAL

(ALL 3 SPOTS TO RUN IN SAME HALF HOUR.   THIS RUNS FIRST.)

LASER VIDEO CASSETTE SPOT #1   (LIVE)

ON MARCH ___ 1984 A NEW CHAPTER IN THE ANNALS OF OFFSHORE RADIO
BEGAN.   LASER 558 STARTED TRANSMISSIONS OF HIT MUSIC RADIO FROM
ABOARD THE M.V. COMMUNICATOR IN THE NORTH SEA.   TO ANNOUNCE THE
BIG EVENT TO THE PRESS WE'VE PRODUCED A LIMITED EDITION SOUVENIR
VIDEO IN COLOR.

ALL THE SHOOTING WAS DONE IN FLORIDA WHILE THE COMMUNICATOR RADIO
SHIP WAS GETTING READY FOR THE TRIP ACROSS THE ATLANTIC. ALTHOUGH
THIS WAS PRODUCED FOR THE PRESS, WE THOUGHT SOME OF OUR LISTENERS
WOULD WANT A COPY FOR HOME VIEWING ON A 15 MINUTE VHS OR BETA
CASSETTE.

YOU CAN ORDER YOUR VERY OWN COPY OF THIS LIMITED EDITION VIDEO
CASSETTE NOW.   SEE ALL THE LASER DEEJAYS GO THROUGH THEIR ANTICS
ABOARD THE M.V. COMMUNICATOR ... ALL TO THE BEAT OF AN ORIGINAL
RAP ROUTINE.

THIS VIDEO CASSETTE WILL SOON BECOME A COLLECTORS' ITEM.   STAY
TUNED, AFTER THE NEXT FEW RECORDS I'LL TELL YOU HOW TO ORDER
YOUR OWN LASER VIDEO CASSETTE.

LASER 558   ALL EUROPE RADIO   OPERATIONS MANUAL

(ALL 3 SPOTS TO RUN IN SAME HALF HOUR.   THIS RUNS SECOND)

LASER VIDEO CASSETTE SPOT #2   (LIVE)

BEFORE THE LAST COUPLE OF RECORDS I WAS TELLING YOU ABOUT THE
SOUVENIR EDITION VIDEO CASSETTE WE'VE PRODUCED ABOUT LASER 558.
ORIGINALLY WE PRODUCED IT FOR THE PRESS, BUT WE THOUGHT SOME OF
OUR LISTENERS WOULD WANT A COPY FOR HOME VIEWING ON A 15 MINUTE
VHS OR BETA CASSETTE.

SEND YOUR NAME AND ADDRESS ALONG WITH A BANKERS DRAFT OR A
CASHIERS CHECK FOR 15 POUNDS STERLING MADE OUT TO:

                    MUSIC MEDIA INTERNATIONAL, INC.

                    341 MADISON AVENUE

                    NEW YORK, NEW YORK 10017 USA

A BANKERS DRAFT OR CASHIERS CHECK CAN BE PURCHASED AT ANY BANK.
ALLOW FOUR WEEKS FOR DELIVERY.   REMEMBER THIS LIMITED EDITION
LASER CASSETTE WILL SOON BECOME A COLLECTORS' ITEM.   DO NOT SEND
PERSONAL CHECKS, MONEY ORDERS OR TRAVELERS CHECKS.   BECAUSE OF
LONG COLLECTION DELAYS, THESE CANNOT BE ACCEPTED.   WE'LL SEND YOU
THE COMPATIBLE SYSTEM FOR TV SETS IN YOUR COUNTRY, BUT INDICATE
WHETHER YOU HAVE A VHS OR BETA RECORDER.

FOR EACH VIDEO SEND A BANKERS DRAFT OR A CASHIERS CHECK FOR 15
POUNDS STERLING TO:

                    MUSIC MEDIA INTERNATIONAL, INC.

                    341 MADISON AVENUE

                    NEW YORK, NEW YORK 10017 USA

ORDER YOUR SOUVENIR LASER 558 VIDEO CASSETTE TODAY!

LASER 558   ALL EUROPE RADIO   OPERATIONS MANUAL

(ALL 3 SPOTS TO RUN IN SAME HALF HOUR.   THIS RUNS THIRD.)

LASER VIDEO CASSETTE SPOT #3   (LIVE)

HERE'S   MORE INFORMATION ON THE LASER VIDEO CASSETTE OFFER YOU'VE
BEEN HEARING ABOUT.
WE'VE   PRODUCED A VIDEO CASSETTE IN COLOR ABOUT LASER 558.   SEE
THE DEEJAYS GO THROUGH THEIR ANTICS ABOARD THE M.V. COMMUNICATOR
RADIO SHIP ... ALL TO THE BEAT OF AN ORIGINAL RAP ROUTINE.   WE
ORIGINALLY PUT THIS TOGETHER FOR THE PRESS ONLY, BUT NOW WE'RE
OFFERING IT TO LISTENERS AS WELL.

THIS LIMITED EDITION SOUVENIR CASSETTE WILL SOON BECOME A
COLLECTOR'S ITEM.   SEND YOUR NAME AND ADDRESS ALONG WITH A
BANKERS DRAFT OR CASHIERS CHECK FOR 15 POUNDS STERLING PAYABLE TO
                    MUSIC MEDIA INTERNATIONAL, INC.
                    341 MADISON AVENUE
                    NEW YORK, NEW YORK 10017 USA
A BANKERS DRAFT OR CASHIERS CHECK CAN BE PURCHASED AT ANY BANK.
ALLOW   FOUR WEEKS FOR DELIVERY.   WE'LL SEND YOU THE COMPATIBLE
SYSTEM FOR TV SETS IN YOUR COUNTRY, BUT INDICATE IF YOU HAVE A
VHS OR BETA RECORDER.   DO NOT SEND PERSONAL CHECKS, MONEY ORDERS
OR TRAVELERS CHECKS.   BECAUSE OF LONG COLLECTION DELAYS THESE
CANNOT BE ACCEPTED.   FOR EACH VIDEO SEND A BANKERS DRAFT OR A
CASHIERS CHECK FOR 15 POUNDS STERLING TO:
                    MUSIC MEDIA INTERNATIONAL, INC.
                    341 MADISON AVENUE
                    NEW YORK, NEW YORK 10017 USA
ORDER YOUR SOUVENIR LASER 558 VIDEO CASSETTE TODAY!

LASER 558   ALL EUROPE RADIO   OPERATIONS MANUAL

L A S E R   558

BROADCASTING STANDARDS

LASER 558 IS OWNED AND OPERATED BY DEKA OVERSEAS AND BROADCASTS IN A '
TOTALLY FREE ENVIRONMENT BEYOND GOVERNMENT REGULATIONS. HOWEVER, AT
ALL TIMES THE STATION WILL BE GOVERNED BY GENERAL STANDARDS OF GOOD
TASTE AND COMMON SENSE.

THESE GUIDELINES ARE NOT ALL INCLUSIVE, BUT ARE DESIGNED TO PROVIDE
GUIDANCE FOR SALES AND OPERATING PERSONNEL IN DEALING WITH SOME OF
THE MOST COMMON SITUATIONS WHICH ARISE CONCERNING ADVERTISING CON-
TINUITY ACCEPTANCE. SECTION A COVERS COMMERCIAL ADVERTISING STANDARDS;
SECTION B COVERS GENERAL PROGRAMMING STANDARDS.

LASER 558   ALL EUROPE RADIO   OPERATIONS MANUAL

SECTION   A

COMMERCIAL ADVERTISING STANDARDS

LASER 558   ALL EUROPE RADIO   OPERATIONS MANUAL

1.   CONTROVERSIAL ISSUES

No advertising will be accepted which obviously addresses and advocates a point of view on a controversial issue of public importance.

2.   DIRECT REPONSE ACCOUNTS

Direct response business requesting that money be sent to the station is acceptable, provided the client sets up and services a box number, supplies the station with 25 to 50 of the item being offered to be used to satisfy complaints, and an appropriate letter of indemnity is signed by an officer of the company and sent to the station. The length of time required to fill the order should be included in the copy: e.g. "four to six weeks delivery", in order to avoid calls to the station that the merchandise has not been received.

3.   OTHER MEDIA ADVERTISING

Advertising of other media will be accepted.

4.   PER INQUIRY ACCOUNTS

"Per Inquiry" business is acceptable only from reputable agencies specializing in the field.

5.   PITCHMAN ACCOUNTS

"Pitchman" type announcements are acceptable only with the approval of the Production Manager. No commercial or commercial break is to be longer than one minute.

6.   BAIT AND SWITCH ADVERTISING

Station will not air so-called "bait and switch" advertising,where the goods or services advertised are not actually going to be sold but are merely a lure to attract the customer for the purpose of selling higher priced substitutes.

7.   HORSE RACING AND SPORTS EVENTS

Announcements and advertising for racing parks or sports events is acceptable provided it does not unduly exhort the public to bet.

LASER 558   ALL EUROPE RADIO   OPERATIONS MANUAL

8.   MEDICAL PRODUCTS ADVERTISING

The advertising of medical products presents considerations of an intimate and far-reaching importance to the consumer, and the following guideline shall apply in the advertising thereof:

(a)   Advertising material which offensively describes or dramatizes distressful or morbid situations involving ailments, by words or effects, is not acceptable;

(b)   Claims that a product will effect a cure, and the use of such words as "safe", "without risk", "harmless" or terms of similar meaning, are not acceptable when used alone. However, such words may become acceptable when used with qualifying words, such as "when taken as directed";

(c)   Extreme care shall be taken to prevent the publicizing of any product which exercises a deleterious effect on the user. The advertising of proprietary medicines and drugs shall be closely supervised to guard against misleading or alarming information, exaggerated claims of efficiency or any possibility of misconception by the public regarding such products;

(d)   Advertising for sleep-inducing preparations shall not be scheduled in or adjacent to children's or teen age programming;

9.   ADVERTISING FOR PROFESSIONAL SERVICES

The following guidelines apply to advertising on behalf of professional practitioners, including but not limtied to medical doctors, dentists, chiropractors and attorneys, including individuals, clinics and similar organizations:

(a)   All aspects of such advertising must conform to governmental regulations;

(b)   Advertising should be designed to convey information which is accurate and relevant to the selection of an individual practitioner by a layperson;

(c)   Stringent standards of taste and the usual high standards of copy documentation will be applied;

(d)   All such advertising must be presented in a restrained manner, without "hard sell" techniques or flamboyant or sensational copy. Self-laudatory claims, and claims disparaging other practitioners in the same field, or making comparisons with them, their work or their fees, are impermissible. Claims creating false expectations as to results or guaranteeing a desired outcome are not permitted;

(e) Misleading or ambiguous language will not be accepted;

(f) Copy must not play upon fears or insecurities;

(g) The advertising may not tie in, or promote, any services or products other than the professional services being advertised;

(h) Advertising may not give the appearance of itself rendering a professional opinion, including an opinion as to whether or not professional advice should be sought;

(i) Content may include any of the following:

    (1) Basic factual information--e.g. name or names; addresses; telephone and telex numbers and office hours; number of practitioners and professional associates; date and place of birth; schools attended and degrees; memberships in professional associations; professional fraternal societies; foreign language ability;

    (2) Information about the practice--e.g. listing one or more fields of their profession in which the person or persons practices or concentrates, including board certifications and areas of specialization;

    (3) Proof may be required of any statements in (1) and (2) above.

(j) Fees and financial arrangements:

    (1) Advertising may quote or refer to fees for consultation or specific services, but must include either (1) a minimum and maximum range for the service or services quoted, (2) other suitable qualifying words which make it clear that total fees may be more than those quoted or (3) if an exact consultation fee is quoted, it must also state the length of time of the consultation;

    (2) Advertising may announce that a written schedule of fees and costs for specific services is available upon request;

    (3) Credit arrangements--e.g. credit cards accepted. If advertising indicates that credit is available, all significant terms of credit arrangements must be described.

LASER 558   ALL EUROPE RADIO   OPERATIONS MANUAL

10.   FALSE OR MISLEADING ADVERTISING

STATION\ will not broadcast commercials which make false or
misleading claims through demonstration or copy, or commercials which misrepresent or exaggerate the value a prospective customer might reasonably expect to secure from the
purchase of the advertised product or service.

11.   ADVERTISING/NEWS

The station shall exercise particular discretion in the
acceptance, placement and presentation of advertising in
news programs, so that such advertising may be clearly
distinguishable from news content. They will also reject
advertising which simulates news techniques.

12.   LOUD COMMERCIALS

Under no circumstances shall an employee of the STATION, be
a party to any action increasing or agreeing to increase the
loudness of any commercial message, live or recorded.

(a) Commercials which appear to present problems of loudness,
     will be either corrected or rejected;

(b) Sales personnel in the course of contract with advertising
     agencies and advertisers, must be sure that there is no
     misunderstanding of our position on this matter.

13.   SPONSORSHIP IDENTIFICATION

Care will be taken to ensure that all commercials are readily
identified as such. Special attention will be given to paid
announcements for entities which do not involve commercial
products or services. Such announcements will likely require
the use of the phrases "paid for by..." or "sponsored by...".
"Teaser" announcements which do not identify the advertiser
are strictly forbidden.

14.   DISPARAGEMENT

Advertising should offer a product or service on its positive
merits and refrain by identification or other means from dis-
crediting, disparaging or unfairly attacking competitors,
competing products, other industries, professions or insti-
tutions.

15.   MOVIE ADVERTISING

We must apply rigorous standards of continuity acceptance to
commercial movies. We must be sure that movie advertisements
are truthful, that they do not seem to be produced with an
implied leer or a suggestive wink, and that they do not dwell
on violence or horror for its own sake.

16.   USE OF THE WORD "FREE" AND"GUARANTEE"

(a)   Use of the word "free" in advertising:

    (1)   The lawfulness of an offer of "free" goods in
connection with a merchandising plan depends on
the terms of the offer and the underlying and
surrounding facts. When the free article is
given only upon the purchase of another article,
the word "free" may be used only under the following circumstances:

        (A)   When all conditions, obligations or other
prerequisites to the receipt and retention
of the free article of merchandise or service
offered are clearly and conspicuously set
forth at the outset so as to leave no reasonable probability that the terms of the offer
will be misunderstood, and regardless of
such disclosure;

        (B)   When, with respect to any article of merchandise
required to be purchased in order to obtain the
free article or service, the offerer (1) has not
increased the ordinary and usual price of such
article of merchandise, (2) reduced the quality
or (3) reduced the quantity or size thereof.

    (2)   The station shall determine compliance with 1(A)
above, and unless clearly apparent, shall obtain
written assurance from the advertiser of compliance
with 1(B);

(b)   Use of the word "guarantee" in advertising:

    (1)   If any advertising copy contains a guarantee or
reference to a guarantee of the product or service
advertised, the station shall require that a copy
of the full written guarantee applying to the product
or service be furnished to it, sufficiently in advance of broadcast to permit its careful review;

LASER 558   ALL EUROPE RADIO   OPERATIONS MANUAL

(2) The broadcast material shall be compared to the full written guarantee to ensure that the former does not mislead;

17.   USE OF THE WORD "SALE"

When the word "sale" appears in a commercial it means that the advertiser is making his products or services available for a limited period of time (usually no more than 30 days), at a price which is lower than his regular established price for the same product or service.

18.   FINANCE CHARGES

Simply stating that "financing is available" is acceptable. However, the mention of any term requires that certain other terms also be disclosed. There are two types of credit advertising--"open end credit" and "closed end credit."

(a) Advertising for "open end credit", such as revolving charge account or a credit card, must contain all of the following if any one term is mentioned:

(1) Any minimum, fixed, transaction, activity or similar charge that could be imposed;

(2) Any periodic interest charge that may be applied, expressed as an annual percentage;

(3) Any membership or participation fee that could be imposed.

(b) Advertising offering "closed end credit", such as the financing of a single item, must contain all of the following if any one term is mentioned:

(1) The cash price of the item or the amount of the loan;

(2) The amount of the down payment, if any;

(3) The number, amount and dates of payments;

(4) The rate-of-finance charge, expressed as an annual percentage.

LASER 558   ALL EUROPE RADIO   OPERATIONS MANUAL

19. LOTTERIES

Lotteries which are advertised in any other medium are acceptable provided they are run by entities outside the U.K. and E.E.C. countries.

20. CHILDREN AND ADVERTISING

Commercials directed at children will be carefully reviewed to be sure that they do not take advantage of children and their special vulnerability.

21. TESTIMONIALS

Persons giving testimonials in commercials must tell the exact truth; that is, they must be actual users of the product or service being advertised and they must describe their actual experience associated with such use.

22. EXCLUSIVITY

No mention must ever be made that any product or service is advertising solely on the station, or that any offer is made only to the station's listeners. This claim is difficult to prove and can only cause possible legal problems.

23. QUALIFICATION OF ADVERTISERS

Multinational companies based outside U.K. and E.E.C. nations commit no offence by advertising on an offshore radio station if schedules are placed through Music Media International in New York and certain other procedures are followed. Counsel's advice and opinion available on request.

Advertising schedules originating from within the U.K. or other E.E.C. nations are not acceptable.

LASER 558   ALL EUROPE RADIO   OPERATIONS MANUAL

SECTION   B

GENERAL PROGRAMMING STANDARDS

1.   OVERALL PROGRAMMING POLICY

The basic aim of the station is to entertain the greatest
number of listeners within the coverage area through a
contemporary hit music format.

2.   MORE MUSIC EMPHASIS

Deejay personalities will present approximately 54 minutes
of music each hour, or about 15 records. News, commercial
advertisements and talk will be held to a minimum so that
listeners will never be more than a minute away from music.

3.   RECORD SELECTION

The music library will be supplied, cataloged and maintained
by a reputable independent music consulting service in New
York. No records are to be added or deleted from their list
without their consent and approval.

4.   FOREIGN LANGUAGES

All of the programming will be in English. However, hit
records in other languages will be played if they have Pan-
European appeal in the opinion of the music consulting service.
On an occasional basis station may air recorded commercial
advertising or promotional announcements which contain some
phrases from another language.

5.   NEWS AND INFORMATION

News will be limited to one-minute of headlines on the hour.
No writing, editing or presentation should indicate explicitly
or implicitly any particular political or controversial view.

Deejays, in their comments between records, should avoid any
political, religious and controversial subjects whatsoever.
Suggestive, profane or disrespectful language should be
avoided as well.

LASER 558 ALL EUROPE RADIO OPERATIONS MANUAL

6. ADVERTISING

Commercial spots or advertisements will be limited to 6 one-minute breaks per hour. Only one minute and half minute commercials will be accepted and they may be recorded or delivered live. For more details see Section A.

7. RELIGIOUS AND OTHER PROGRAMMING

Religious programs up to one hour in length are acceptable in specified hours for this purpose.

8. PROGRAMMING FROM OUTSIDE SOURCES

No programming content supplied from outside sources (other than the independent music consulting service and any religious program service) is acceptable.

9. GEOGRAPHICAL EMPHASIS

No programming should be directed to any specific country, but to the coverage area as a whole.

10. WEATHER

Because of the broad coverage area of the station, weather reports and forecasts are to be avoided, so as not to confuse listeners.

11. TIME

Since the station can be received in two time zones, if the hour is given, it should be given as GMT first, then Continental Time which is one hour later.

12. OTHER POLICY MATTERS

The station operations manager will have the authority to decide on all other policy matters not put forth in this document.

23412486R00102

Printed in Great Britain
by Amazon